D0418030

Microsoft Access 2007
explained

Books Available

By the same authors:

BP590	Microsoft Access 2007 explained
BP585	Microsoft Excel 2007 explained
BP584	Microsoft Word 2007 explained
BP583	Microsoft Office 2007 explained
BP581	Windows Vista explained
BP580	Windows Vista for Beginners
BP569	Microsoft Works 8.0 & Works Suite 2006 explained
BP563	Using Windows XP's Accessories
BP558	Microsoft Works 8.0 & Works Suite 2005 explained
BP557	How Did I Do That ... in Windows XP
BP555	Using PDF Files
BP550	Advanced Guide to Windows XP
BP548	Easy PC Keyboard Shortcuts
BP546	Microsoft Works Suite 2004 explained
BP545	Paint Shop Pro 8 explained
BP544	Microsoft Office 2003 explained
BP538	Windows XP for Beginners
BP525	Controlling Windows XP the easy way
BP522	Microsoft Works Suite 2002 explained
BP514	Windows XP explained
BP513	IE 6 and Outlook Express 6 explained
BP512	Microsoft Access 2002 explained
BP511	Microsoft Excel 2002 explained
BP510	Microsoft Word 2002 explained
BP509	Microsoft Office XP explained
BP498	Using Visual Basic
BP493	Windows Me explained
BP491	Windows 2000 explained
BP487	Quicken 2000 UK explained
BP486	Using Linux the easy way
BP465	Lotus SmartSuite Millennium explained
BP433	Your own Web site on the Internet
BP341	MS-DOS explained
BP284	Programming in QuickBASIC
BP258	Learning to Program in C

Microsoft Access 2007 explained

by

P.R.M. Oliver
and
N. Kantaris

Bernard Babani (publishing) Ltd
The Grampians
Shepherds Bush Road
London W6 7NF
England
www.babanibooks.com

Please Note

Although every care has been taken with the production of this book to ensure that any projects, designs, modifications and/or programs, etc., contained herewith, operate in a correct and safe manner and also that any components specified are normally available in Great Britain, the Publishers and Author(s) do not accept responsibility in any way for the failure (including fault in design) of any project, design, modification or program to work correctly or to cause damage to any equipment that it may be connected to or used in conjunction with, or in respect of any other damage or injury that may be so caused, nor do the Publishers accept responsibility in any way for the failure to obtain specified components.

Notice is also given that if equipment that is still under warranty is modified in any way or used or connected with home-built equipment then that warranty may be void.

© 2008 BERNARD BABANI (publishing) LTD

First Published – February 2008

British Library Cataloguing in Publication Data:

A catalogue record for this book is available from the British Library

ISBN 978 0 85934 590 3

Cover Design by Gregor Arthur
Printed and Bound in Great Britain by J. H. Haynes & Co. Ltd., Sparkford

About this Book

Microsoft Access 2007 explained has been written to help users to get to grips with Microsoft's new relational database *Access* 2007, part of the *Microsoft Office 2007* package, specifically designed for both the *Windows Vista* and *Windows XP* environments.

Microsoft Access 2007 is an exciting new program that will help with the new demands, challenges and opportunities to both individuals and business. It has a completely new interface which replaces the menus, toolbars and most of the task panes and dialogue boxes of previous versions, with a ribbon of buttons organised into themed tabs, a Quick Access toolbar that you can customise with commands you use the most, and just one menu.

Access 2007 provides a powerful set of tools that allow you to quickly start tracking, reporting, and sharing information in a manageable environment. It allows you to rapidly create attractive and functional databases without requiring deep database knowledge. You can use the 'Getting Started with Microsoft Office Access' page to quickly create a database from scratch, or start with one of the professionally designed database templates.

The package incorporates several new features, as well as improvements on its previous capabilities, including:

- The new Ribbon in Access 2007 groups tools by task, and the commands you use most frequently are close at hand. This new, results-oriented interface presents tools to you when you need them.

- Creating tables is now easier — just click Table on the Create tab and start entering data.

- Two new views let you work with forms and reports interactively. Report view adds the ability to browse, but Layout view lets you make design changes while you browse.

- Access 2007 includes new and enhanced data types and controls that allow you to enter and store more types of data. You can create a field that holds multiple values, or complex data. The new Attachment data type lets you easily store all types of documents and image files in your database without any unnecessary growth in database size. Memo fields now store rich text and support revision history.

- With the new rich text support in Access 2007 you are no longer limited to plain text in your records. You can format text as bold or italic for instance, and use different fonts and colours.

- Fields and controls using the Date/Time data type now get a new built-in interactive calendar for choosing dates.

- Datasheet view now has a 'Total' row, in which you can display a sum, count, average, maximum, minimum, standard deviation, or variance.

- Access 2007 lets you export data to a PDF (Portable Document Format) or XPS (XML Paper Specification) file format for printing, posting, and e-mail distribution, but you need extra free software to do this.

- Access 2007 macros have been completely redesigned. They can be more powerful but are still fairly easy to create in the new Macro Builder.

No previous knowledge is assumed, but the book does not describe how to install and use Microsoft Windows itself. If you need to know more about Windows, then may we suggest you select a book from the 'Books Available' list published by BERNARD BABANI (publishing) Ltd.

Microsoft Access 2007 explained was written using both Windows Vista and Windows XP. The only real differences, as far as the book is concerned, being that Vista's **Start** menu does not cascade, its window frames, by default, are semi transparent, and it uses Vista's newly designed system dialogue boxes.

This book introduces Access 2007 with sufficient detail to get you working on your own databases, then discusses how to use the new rich text formatting features, how to build and customise good looking forms and reports, and how to get started with the new macros. No prior knowledge of the package's capabilities is assumed.

The book was written with the busy person in mind. It is not necessary to learn all there is to know about a subject, when reading a few selected pages can usually do the same thing quite adequately.

Using this book, it is hoped that you will be able to come to terms with Microsoft Access 2007 and get the most out of your computer in terms of efficiency, productivity and enjoyment, and that you will be able to do it in the shortest, most effective and informative way. Good luck.

About the Authors

Phil Oliver graduated in Mining Engineering at Camborne School of Mines in 1967 and since then has specialised in most aspects of surface mining technology, with a particular emphasis on computer related techniques. He has worked in Guyana, Canada, several Middle Eastern and Asian countries, South Africa and the United Kingdom, on such diverse projects as: the planning and management of bauxite, iron, gold and coal mines; rock excavation contracting in the UK; international mining equipment sales and international mine consulting. In 1988 he took up a lecturing position at Camborne School of Mines (part of Exeter University) in Surface Mining and Management. He retired from this in 1998, to spend more time writing, consulting and developing Web sites for clients.

Noel Kantaris graduated in Electrical Engineering at Bristol University and after spending three years in the Electronics Industry in London, took up a Tutorship in Physics at the University of Queensland. Research interests in Ionospheric Physics, led to the degrees of M.E. in Electronics and Ph.D. in Physics. On return to the UK, he took up a Post-Doctoral Research Fellowship in Radio Physics at the University of Leicester, and then in 1973 a lecturing position in Engineering at the Camborne School of Mines, Cornwall, (part of Exeter University), where between 1978 and 1997 he was also the CSM IT Manager. At present he is IT Director of FFC Ltd.

Acknowledgements

We would like to thank friends and colleagues, for their helpful tips and suggestions which assisted us in the writing of this book.

Trademarks

Arial and **Times New Roman** are registered trademarks of The Monotype Corporation plc.

HP and LaserJet are registered trademarks of Hewlett Packard Corporation.

IBM is a registered trademark of International Business Machines, Inc.

Intel is a registered trademark of Intel Corporation.

Calibri, **Cambria**, **Excel**, **IntelliMouse**, **Microsoft**, **MS-DOS**, **Office logo**, **Outlook**, **PowerPoint**, **SmartArt**, **Visual Basic** and **Windows**, are either registered trademarks or trademarks of Microsoft Corporation.

PostScript is a registered trademark of Adobe Systems Incorporated.

TrueType is a registered trademark of Apple Corporation.

All other brand and product names and logos used in the book are recognised as trademarks, or registered trademarks, of their respective companies.

Contents

1

Package Overview

Microsoft's Access 2007 is a database management system (DBMS) designed to allow you to store, manipulate and retrieve information easily and quickly. It is part of the Office 2007 package and is without doubt the best Office database so far. It is fully integrated with all the other Office 2007 applications.

A database is a collection of data that exists and is organised around a specific theme or requirement. Databases can be of the 'flat-file' type, or can have relational capabilities, as in the case of Access, which is known as a relational database management system (RDBMS). What a mouthful!

The main difference between flat-file and relational database systems is that the latter can store and manipulate data in multiple 'tables', while the former systems can only manipulate a single table at any given time. To make accessing the data easier, each row (or record) of data within a database table is structured in the same fashion, i.e., each record will have the same number of columns (or fields).

We define a database and its various elements as:

Database	A collection of data organised for a specific theme in one or more tables.
Table	A two-dimensional structure in which data is stored, like in a spreadsheet.
Record	A row of information in a table relating to a single entry and comprising one or more fields.
Field	A single column of information of the same type, such as people's names.

In Access 2007 the maximum size of a database is 2 gigabytes and can include linked tables in other files. The number of objects in a database is limited to 32,768, while the maximum number of fields in a table is limited to 255.

A good example of a flat-file database would be the invoicing details kept on its clients by a company. These details could include name of client, description of work done, invoice number, and amount charged, something like the following:

NAME	Consultancy	Invoice	Value
VORTEX Co. Ltd	Wind Tunnel Tests	0401	120.84
AVON Construction	Adhesive Tests	0402	103.52
BARROWS Associates	Tunnel Design Tests	0403	99.32
STONEAGE Ltd	Carbon Dating Tests	0404	55.98
PARKWAY Gravel	Material Size Tests	0405	180.22
WESTWOOD Ltd	Load Bearing Tests	0406	68.52

Fig. 1.1 An Example of a Flat-File Database

Such a flat-file DBMS is too limited for the type of information normally held by most companies. If the same client asks for work to be carried out regularly, then the details for that client (which could include address, e-mail and Web site details, telephone and fax numbers, contact name, date of invoice, etc.), will have to be entered several times. This can lead to errors, but above all to redundant information being kept on a client, as each entry would have to have the name of the client, their address, telephone and fax numbers.

The relational facilities offered by Access, overcome the problems of entry errors and duplication of information. The ability to handle multiple tables at any one time allows for the grouping of data into sensible subsets. For example, one table, called client, could hold the names of the clients, their addresses, telephone and fax numbers, while another table, called invoice, could hold information on the work done, invoice number, date of issue, and amount charged.

The two tables must, however, have one unique common field, such as a client reference number. The advantage is that details of each client are entered and stored only once, thus reducing the time and effort wasted on entering duplicate information, and also reducing the space required for data storage.

Access 2007 uses Object Linking and Embedding (OLE) to move and share information seamlessly between Office applications. For example, you can drag information from one application to another, or you can link information from one application into another.

Once you get used to the new interface, you will find using Access 2007 to be even more intuitive and easy than earlier versions.

The New 2007 Interface

Access 2007 has a built-in consistency with the other applications that make up Office 2007 which makes them easier to use. Previous releases used a system of menus, toolbars, task panes, and dialogue boxes to access commands and get things done.

Because Microsoft Office 2007 programs do so much more, these features have been replaced with a new user interface which makes it easier to find and use the full range of features they provide. This is somewhat daunting at first, but once you start using the new interface you will very rapidly get used to it. We did anyway!

As we shall see, when Access is first opened the initial screen is similar to that of Publisher 2007 but very different from the other Office 2007 programs. Although Access 2007 does use the new interface, it does not show the Ribbon until a database is actually open.

The Ribbon

Traditional menus and toolbars have been replaced by the Ribbon – a new device that presents commands organised into a set of tabs.

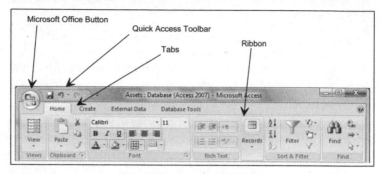

Fig. 1.2 The Access 2007 Ribbon

The tabs on the Ribbon display the commands that are most relevant for each of the task areas in the applications, as shown above. Contextual tabs also appear when they are needed so that you can very easily find and use the commands needed for the operation that is current. As an example, selecting **Design View** from the **Home**, **View** drop-down list, opens the **Design** contextual tab on the Ribbon with commands used for designing database objects. Once you leave Design View, this tab disappears.

Fig. 1.2 above also shows two of the other new features of Access 2007. These are:

The Microsoft Office Button

 The Microsoft Office Button (or **Office Button** as we shall call it), replaces the **File** menu of previous versions and is located in the upper-left corner of the Access window.

When you click this button you see commands such as **New**, **Open**, **Save** and **Print** your file, as well as new commands such as **Manage, E-mail** and **Publish**. The right side of the menu lists your recently opened documents, and gives access to the Access control options.

Quick Access Toolbar

The Quick Access Toolbar is the small area to the upper left of the Ribbon, as shown in Fig. 1.2. This bar contains buttons for the things that you use over and over every day, such as **Save**, **Undo**, and **Repeat**. It is very easy to add your favourite commands to it so that they are available no matter which tab you are on.

These and the other new features of the Access 2007 user interface are described in more detail in the next chapter.

How to Get Classic Menus

If you really can't come to terms with the new 2007 interface, there is at least one way to get the classic menus and toolbars back, as an add-in which you can download from:

www.addintools.com/english/menuaccess/

We haven't done it ourselves, but you can download and install this software and "you will see and enjoy the classic menu and toolbars of Access 2003 in Access 2007". At less than £10.00 it could be worth a try, but a retrograde step!

Hardware and Software Requirements

Access 2007 is part of Microsoft Office 2007, so if this is already installed on your computer, you can safely skip this and the next section of this chapter.

The minimum requirements for Office 2007 are an IBM-compatible PC with a processor of at least 500 MHz, (1 gigahertz (GHz) processor or higher for Outlook with Business Contact Manager), 256 MB of RAM and 2 GB of hard disc space. 512 MB of RAM or higher is recommended for Outlook with Business Contact Manager. Some of the hard disc space will be freed after installation if the original download package is removed from the hard drive.

In addition you will require:

- Microsoft Windows XP with Service Pack (SP) 2, Windows Server 2003 with SP1, or later operating system (such as Windows Vista).

- A CD-ROM or DVD drive.

- 1024x768 or higher resolution monitor.

- Connectivity to Microsoft Exchange Server 2000 or later is required for certain advanced functionality in Outlook 2007. Connectivity to Microsoft Windows Server 2003 with SP1 or later running Microsoft Windows SharePoint Services is required for certain advanced collaboration functionality. Microsoft Office SharePoint Server 2007 is required for certain advanced functionality. As far as this book is concerned, none of these are required!

- To share data among multiple computers, the host computer must be running Windows Server 2003 with SP1, Windows XP Professional with SP2, or later.

- Microsoft Internet Explorer 6.0 or later, 32-bit browser only.

- Internet functionality requires access to the Internet.

Obtaining Access 2007

At the time of writing, Access 2007 was available as a stand-alone database for about £175, or as part of the Professional (or higher) edition of Office 2007 (for a little less than £400).

With the latter you also get the 2007 versions of Word, Excel, Powerpoint, Publisher and Outlook.

Downloading Office 2007

Perhaps the easiest way to get started with Access 2007 is to download a free 60-day trial version of Office 2007.

At the time of writing this could be done from the following Web address:

http://ukireland.trymicrosoftoffice.com/

For us this opened the window shown in Fig. 1.3 below.

Fig. 1.3 Downloading a Version of Office 2007

We clicked the **Try Now** button against Office Professional 2007 and had to log in to Windows Live ID. Once this was done the download page was presented. We made a note of the Microsoft Office Product Key and clicked both the **Download** buttons, choosing to save the files to a new folder on our hard drive. In fact the key was also sent to us in an e-mail from Microsoft.

The downloads, at 635MB, were very large and took time enough for a shower and several mugs of coffee, but our selected folder then contained two new files.

- X12-30196.exe – This was 388 MB and contained the 2007 Office suite.

- X13-11296.exe – This was 247 MB and only contained the Business Contact Manager add-in.

Trial Conditions

To start a trial, once you have installed it (as described in the next section) you must activate the trial software over the Internet. The activation process begins automatically when you open any Microsoft Office 2007 product for the first time. If you prefer, you can bypass the activation and launch Office 2007 applications up to 25 times before you need to enter the Product Key and activate the package.

Before the trial period ends you will start receiving reminders saying when the trial will end. If you click the **Convert** button in one of these message windows, you can convert your trial software to the full licensed version in the Setup Wizard that opens. In the Setup dialogue box, click **Enter Product Key** if you have bought the full product from a retailer, or click **Buy Online Key** if you do not have a perpetual product key and would like to purchase it online.

With the first option, to avoid having to uninstall the trial version and then reinstall the full version make sure that you purchase the same full product version and language as the trial software you used.

After the trial period ends, if you do not buy Office 2007, you can still use the trial version after a fashion, but with the following limitations:

- You will not be able to create any new files.

- You will not be able to modify existing files.

- You will be able to print existing files but not save them.

After launching the full version for the first time you will need to activate it. You can do this over the Internet or by phone. The default option is to activate the software over the Internet. The trial is then converted to perpetual use with no uninstall or reinstall necessary. Good luck!

We will now step through the installation procedure with Windows XP. The operation in Windows Vista is almost the same and we have flagged up any differences.

Installing Microsoft Office 2007

Installing Office on your computer's hard disc is now a fairly painless operation. If you are installing the trial version, locate the file **X12-30196.exe** that you downloaded onto your hard disc, and double-click on it to start the set-up process. Be aware though, that you may have downloaded a different file name, so make sure you make a note of it.

To install Microsoft Office from the box, place the distribution CD in your CD/DVD drive and close it. The auto-start program on the CD should start the SETUP

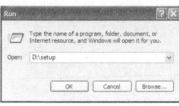

program automatically. If it doesn't, click the **Start** button, and select the **Run** command which opens the Run dialogue box, as shown in Fig. 1.4. Next, type in the **Open** box:

Fig. 1.4 The Run Dialogue Box

D:\setup

In our case the CD/DVD was in the d: drive; yours could be different. Clicking the **OK** button, starts the installation of Microsoft Office 2007. With both methods, SETUP first displays a message box telling you it is extracting files and then opens the Enter your Product Key window, shown in Fig. 1.5 below.

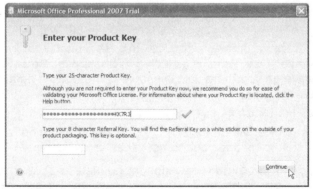

Fig. 1.5 Entering the Product Key

From now on you just follow the instructions given. If you don't enter the Product Key code correctly you will not be able to go further though! Clicking the **Continue** button opens the next window for you to read and accept Microsoft's licence terms.

In the next window, click **Install Now** for a default complete installation of Office 2007, or click **Customize** which gives you some choices.

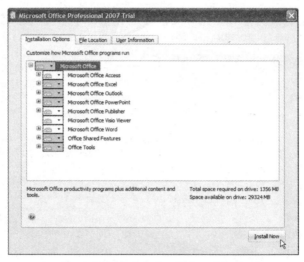

Fig. 1.6 The Installation Options Window

The Installation Options tab, shown open above, lists the Office 2007 applications to be installed and how they will run. You work your way through this list until the type of installation you want is selected. The space required and available on your hard disc is shown in the bottom right of the pane.

The File Location tab lets you set where on your hard disc(s) Office will be installed. The User Information tab lets you enter or change your name, initials and company.

Clicking the **Install Now** button, pointed to above, copies files to your computer's hard disc, sets up the applications and hopefully displays the window shown in Fig. 1.7.

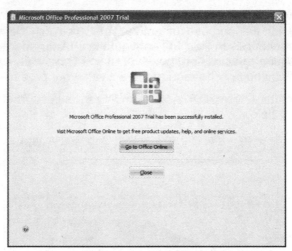

Fig. 1.7 The Successful Installation Window

To start an Office 2007 application, use the **Start**, **All Programs** command and select the **Microsoft Office** entry from the menu, as shown for Windows XP in Fig. 1.8.

Fig. 1.8 The Microsoft Office Cascade Menu

Clicking on one of the Office applications starts the Activation Wizard. During activation, the product ID and a non-unique hardware identification are sent to Microsoft, but it does not include personal information or any data held on your computer. The product ID is generated from the product key used to install the software and a generic code representing the version and language of the Microsoft Office being activated. The non-unique hardware identification represents the configuration of your PC at the time of activation.

The hardware identification identifies only the PC and is used solely for the purpose of activation. Office can detect and accept changes to your PC configuration. Minor upgrades will not require re-activation, however, if you completely overhaul your PC, you may be required to activate your product again.

The first Office 2007 Activation Wizard screen is shown in Fig. 1.9 below.

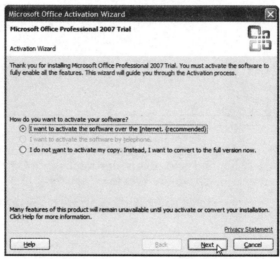

Fig. 1.9 The Office Activation Wizard Screen

As you can see, in this Wizard screen you would normally be able to choose the method of activation; via the Internet, or by telephone. In our case above, we were activating a trial copy so the telephone option was greyed out and not available. If you choose to activate your product through the Internet and you are not already connected, the Wizard will help you get connected.

Note: There is no software registration with the 2007 Office system. Instead, you have the option of registering for special online services from Microsoft Office Online. These include free community-submitted templates and search results tailored to the products you have installed.

Adding or Removing Office Applications

Fig. 1.10 The Windows Start Menu

To add or remove an Office application with Windows XP, left-click the *start* button and click the **Control Panel** option on the Windows pop-up menu, as shown in Fig. 1.10. This opens the Control Panel dialogue box shown in Fig. 1.11.

Next, double-click the **Add/Remove Programs** icon, pointed to in Fig. 1.11 (or **Programs and Features** in Vista) to open the Add or Remove Programs dialogue box shown in Figure 1.12 on the next page.

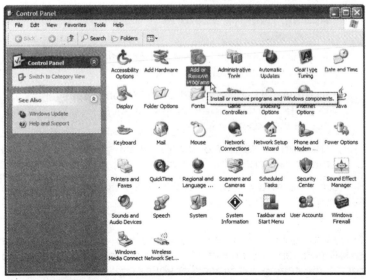

Fig. 1.11 The Control Panel Dialogue Box in Windows XP

Next, locate the Microsoft Office program and click the **Change** button, as shown for Windows XP below. In Windows Vista the **Change** option is in the command bar above the program listing.

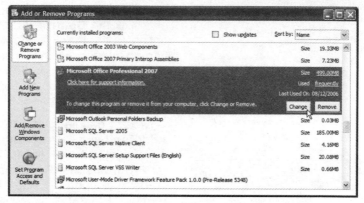

Fig. 1.12 The Add/Remove Programs Dialogue Box

This opens a simple window with options for you to change your installation of Office 2007.

- **Add or Remove Features** – Lets you change your Office setup.

- **Repair** – Reinstalls the whole of Office 2007 to fix any errors in the original installation.

- **Remove** – Uninstalls Office 2007 from your system.
  In Vista the **Uninstall** option is in the command bar above the program listing.

- **Convert** – Available for the Trial version to let you easily convert to the final version.

Selecting the **Add or Remove Features** option and pressing the **Continue** button opens up the dialogue box of Fig. 1.13 on the facing page.

This is similar to the one used for an initial custom installation, shown in Fig. 1.6, but without the options to control the saving destination or your personal information.

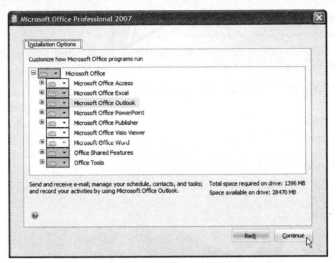

Fig. 1.13 The Installation Options for Office Applications

A plus (+) sign to the left of an application indicates sub-features which you can add or remove from the Office installation by right-clicking it and selecting from the list of options that appear, as shown in Fig. 1.14 below.

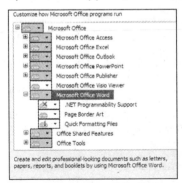

Fig. 1.14 Setting Options for Office Applications

Run from My Computer will install and store a feature on your hard disc. **Run all from My Computer** will also install and store all the sub-features. With **Installed on First Use** the feature will be installed on your hard disc when you use it for the first time. Selecting **Not Available** will remove the feature.

The Mouse Pointers

In Access 2007, as with all other graphical based programs, using a mouse makes many operations both easier and more fun to carry out.

The program makes use of the mouse pointers available in Windows, some of the most common of which are illustrated below. When an Office application is initially started up the first you will see is the hourglass with Windows XP, or the rotating circle with Windows Vista, which turns into an upward pointing hollow arrow once the individual application screen appears on your display. Other shapes depend on the type of work you are doing at the time.

The rotating Vista circle which displays when you are waiting while performing a function.

The XP hourglass which displays when you are waiting while performing a function.

The arrow which appears when the pointer is placed over menus, scrolling bars, and buttons.

The I-beam which appears in normal text areas of the screen. For additional 'Click and Type' pointer shapes, specific to Access, see the table overleaf.

The 4-headed arrow which appears when you choose to move a table, a chart area, or a frame.

The double arrows which appear when over the border of a window, used to drag the side and alter the size of the window.

The Help hand which appears in the Help windows, and is used to access 'hypertext' type links.

Office 2007 applications, like other Windows packages, have additional mouse pointers which facilitate the execution of selected commands. Some of these are:

↓   The vertical pointer which appears when pointing over a column in a table or worksheet and used to select the column.

➡   The horizontal pointer which appears when pointing at a row in a table or worksheet and used to select the row.

⟋   The slanted arrow which appears when the pointer is placed in the selection bar area of text or a table.

◄╫►   The vertical split arrow which appears when pointing over the area separating two columns and used to size a column.

⇕   The horizontal split arrow which appears when pointing over the area separating two rows and used to size a row.

+   The cross which you drag to extend or fill a series.

✎   The draw pointer which appears when you are drawing freehand.

Access has a few additional mouse pointers to the ones above, but their shapes are mostly self-evident.

New Features in Access 2007

Like other Microsoft Office 2007 applications, Access has a cleaner, simpler look to its interface. To quote Microsoft, "It features a streamlined, uncluttered workspace that minimises distraction and enables people to achieve the results they want more quickly and easily". Other changes include:

- The new Ribbon in Access 2007 groups tools by task, and the commands you use most frequently are close at hand. This new, results-oriented interface presents tools to you when you need them.

- Creating tables is now easier — just click Table on the Create tab and start entering data.

- Two new views let you work with forms and reports interactively. Report View adds the ability to browse, but Layout View lets you make design changes while you browse.

- Access 2007 includes new and enhanced data types and controls that allow you to enter and store more types of data. You can create a field that holds multiple values, or complex data. The new Attachment data type lets you easily store all types of documents and binary files in your database without any unnecessary growth in database size. Memo fields now store rich text and support revision history.

- With the new rich text support in Access 2007 you are no longer limited to plain text in your records. You can format text as bold or italic for instance, and use different fonts and colours.

- Fields and controls using the Date/Time data type now get a new built-in interactive calendar for choosing dates.

- Datasheet View now has a Total row, in which you can display a sum, count, average, maximum, minimum, standard deviation, or variance.

- Access 2007 lets you export data to a PDF (Portable Document Format) or XPS (XML Paper Specification) file format for printing, posting, and e-mail distribution, but you need extra software to do this.

Getting Help in Access 2007

No matter how experienced you are, there will always be times when you need help to find out how to do something in Access 2007. There are several ways to get help, but don't look for the Office Assistant, as it has now been switched off for good! We never used it anyway.

The Built-in Microsoft Help System

 All of the Office 2007 applications operate in the same way. If you press the **F1** function key, or click the **Microsoft Office Access Help** button in the top right of the Access screen, shown here, the Help window will open as in Fig. 1.15 below.

Fig. 1.15 The Access Help Window

The program expects you to be 'Online', or connected to the Internet. In fact, if you are not, it will attempt to connect you. You can control where Help searches for its content in two ways. If you click the down arrow to the right of the **Search** button a drop-down menu opens as shown in Fig. 1.15. This has several online and PC based options. If you click the **Access Help** option under **Content from this computer** the Help system will only look on your computer for its help data.

Fig. 1.16 Connection Status Menu

Whether you are looking at **Help** online or offline is shown in the lower-right corner of the Help window, as shown in Fig. 1.16.

Clicking this area with the mouse opens the **Connection Status** menu shown in Fig. 1.16. As can be seen, this offers an easier way to tell **Help** where to look for its content. This setting is retained after you close the Help window, so if you don't want to search online you only have to set this once.

In the Help window the **Table of Contents** list in the left pane opens up a list of available help topics in the form of closed books . Left-clicking one of these books opens it and displays a further list of topics with an icon, as shown in Fig. 1.15.

Clicking any of these opens the relevant Help page in the right-hand pane. We suggest you try looking up 'what's new' as it's an excellent starting point in learning how to use the Access Help System.

If you want to know more about the options in a dialogue box, click the **Help** button in the top right corner of the box. This will open the Help window, which sometimes has relevant help showing in the right-hand pane.

Searching Help

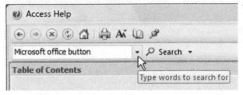

Fig. 1.17 Typing Words to Search For

A quick way to find what you want in the Help system is to enter the text you want to search for in the **Type words to search for** box, as shown here in Fig. 1.17. A search using 2 to 7 words returns the most accurate results. If you want to repeat a search, you click the down arrow to the right of the **Type words to search for** list, and then click the search term that you want in the list.

The Help Toolbar

The buttons on the Help toolbar have the following functions:

Back – Opens the previous Help page viewed in the current session list.

Forward – Opens the next Help page viewed in the current session list.

Stop – Stops loading a document.

Refresh – Re-loads the current Help page.

Home – Opens the first (or Home) Help page for the open application.

Print – Opens the Print dialogue box to let you print all, or a selection, of the current Help topic.

Change Font Size – Opens a sub-menu to let you control the size of text in the Help window.

Hide/Show Table of Contents – A toggle key which closes or reopens the left pane of the Help window, giving more room for the Help text.

Keep On Top/Not On Top – A toggle key you can click to keep the Help window displaying on top of, or below, any open Office 2007 applications.

The Help system is quite comprehensive and it is usually easy to find the information you are looking for. We strongly recommend that you spend some time here to learn about the program. An hour now may well save many hours later!

Screen Tips

If you want to know what a particular button or feature does you can also get Screen Tips help. For information on a particular button or feature, rest the pointer on it and a floating box will appear as shown in Fig. 1.18 below.

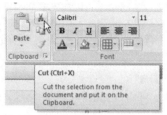

Fig. 1.18 A Typical Screen Tip Floating Box

Here we hovered the pointer over the **Cut** button in the **Clipboard** group and a quite detailed description was given. This feature is much improved in Office 2007 applications.

Access 2007 File Formats

Access 2007 employs a new file format with the **.accdb** file extension that supports a number of product enhancements (including multivalued fields and attachments). When you create a new database in Access 2007 this new file format is used by default.

Earlier versions of Access use the **.mdb** file extension. You can still open **.mdb** files in Access 2007, but you can't then take advantage of the new features that require the new **.accdb** file format.

A database in the new **.accdb** Access 2007 file format cannot be opened by or linked to earlier versions of Access. The new format no longer supports the replication or user-level security features. If you need to use your database with earlier versions of Access, or if you need to use replication or user-level security, you must use a file format from an earlier version. This is easy to do from the **Office Button** menu, shown in Fig. 1.19 below. The **Save As** option lets you save a database in the format of the last two versions of Access.

Fig. 1.19 Saving a Database in an Earlier Version of Access

File Types

We list below a simplified summary of the file types that are used by the Office Access 2007 file format.

.accdb	The standard file name extension for databases in the Access 2007 file format. This format takes the place of the **.mdb** extension used in earlier versions of Access.
.accde	The file name extension for Access 2007 files that are compiled into an "execute only" file. This format takes the place of the **.mde** file name extension used in earlier versions of Access.

An **.accde** file is a "locked" version of the original **.accdb** file. If it contains any Visual Basic for Applications (VBA) code, only the compiled code is included in the **.accde** file and this cannot be viewed or modified by the user. Users also can't make design changes to forms or reports.

.accdt   The file name extension for Access Database Templates.

.accdr   A new file name extension that enables you to open a database in run-time mode. By changing a database's file name extension from **.accdb** to **.accdr**, you can create a "locked" version of your Office Access 2007 database. You can change the file name extension back to **.accdb** to restore full functionality to your database.

2

The New User Interface

Pick and Click

When you open a database in Access 2007 you will notice that the program interface has changed quite dramatically. The menu and toolbar design of previous versions has been replaced with a new user interface to make it easier to find and use all the available commands and features. 'Pick and Click' is very much the order of the day. This is somewhat daunting at first, but once you start using the new interface you will very rapidly get used to it.

The Ribbon

Traditional menus and toolbars have been replaced by the Ribbon – a new device that presents commands organised into a set of tabs, as shown in Fig.2.1 below.

Fig. 2.1 The Home Tab of the Access 2007 Ribbon

The tabs on the Ribbon display the commands that are most relevant for each of the task areas in an application, as shown here for Access 2007. There are four basic components to the Ribbon.

Tabs   There are four basic tabs across the top, each representing an activity area.

Groups   Each tab has several groups that show related items together.

Commands Buttons that you click to action.

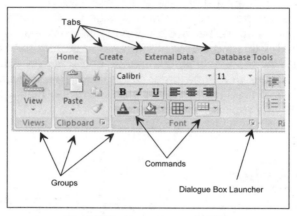

Dialogue Box Launcher – Many groups have an arrow icon in the lower-right corner to open an 'old style' dialogue box.

Fig. 2.2 The Components of a Ribbon

The Home tab contains all the things you use most often, such as setting which **View** is active, the **Cut** and **Paste** commands and those used for formatting, and for changing text font, size, bold, italic, and so on. Clicking a new tab opens a new series of groups, each with its relevant command buttons. This really works very well.

The Ribbon is scalable, and adapts to different sized screens or windows. It displays smaller versions of tabs and groups as screen resolution decreases. When the Ribbon gets smaller, the groups on the open tab begin to shrink with the most commonly used commands left open. Access 2007 is probably best used with large high-resolution screens, but there again, so is almost everything else in computing!

Dialogue Box Launcher

The new Ribbons hold the most commonly used command buttons for the program, but by no means all of the available commands. Some groups have a small diagonal arrow in the lower-right corner.

This is the new **Dialogue Box Launcher**. You click it to see more options related to that group. They often appear as a Dialogue box similar to those of previous versions of Access, as shown in Fig. 2.3 below.

Fig. 2.3 The Datasheet Formatting Dialogue Box (Vista)

This was opened by clicking the **Dialogue Box Launcher** located on the **Font** group of the **Home** tab of the Access 2007 Ribbon.

To confuse matters slightly, some **Dialogue Box Launchers** actually open task panes, not dialogue boxes. Try clicking the Launcher on the **Home**, **Clipboard** group, to see what we mean.

Contextual Tabs

Not all of the available tabs are visible. Some only appear when they are needed. As an example, when you select **Design View** Access opens the **Design** contextual tab on the Ribbon with commands used for designing the current database object, as shown in Fig. 2.4 on the next page .

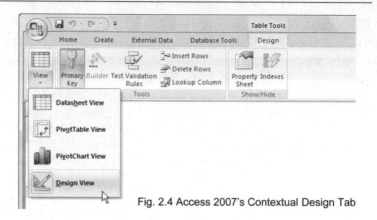

Fig. 2.4 Access 2007's Contextual Design Tab

Hiding the Ribbon

The Ribbon makes everything in Access 2007 centralised and easy to find, but there are times when you just want to work on your document.

You can maximise your working area by hiding the Ribbon. To do this just double-click the active tab. All the groups just disappear. Go on, try it. When you want to see the commands again, double-click the active tab to bring back the groups.

If you find you hate the Ribbon in Access 2007 you have a problem as there is no direct way to delete or replace it with the toolbars and menus from the earlier versions. If you are really desperate you could, however, try the add-in mentioned on page 5. Not having tried this ourselves, we can't recommend it, but it looks to be one solution.

Ribbon Keyboard Shortcuts

Those of you who have trouble using a mouse will be glad to hear that all the Ribbon features are available from the keyboard using what are now called **Key Tips**.

Pressing the **Alt** key makes Key Tip badges appear for all Ribbon tabs, the Quick Access Toolbar commands, and the Microsoft Office Button, as shown in Fig. 2.5 below.

Fig. 2.5 Access 2007 Ribbon Showing Tab Key Tips

Then you can press the Key Tip for the tab you want to display. If that tab is the active one, all the Key Tips for the tab's commands appear, as we show in Fig. 2.6 below, where we pressed the 'H' keyboard key. Then you can press the Key Tip for the command you want.

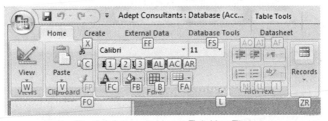

Fig. 2.6 Access's Home Tab Key Tips

When you press a Key Tip for a non-active tab, the tab is opened and all the Key Tips for the tab's commands appear.

Access keys let you quickly use commands by pressing a few keystrokes, no matter where you are in the program. To close them you press the **Alt** key again.

You can still use the old **Alt+** shortcuts that accessed menus and commands in previous versions of Office applications, but because the old menus are no longer available you need to know the full shortcuts to use them.

Shortcuts that start with the **Ctrl** key, such as **Ctrl+C** for copy, remain the same as in previous versions.

The Microsoft Office Button

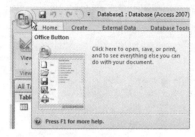

Fig. 2.7 The Office Button Screen Tip

The **Office Button** is in the upper-left corner of most of Access 2007's windows. It replaces the File menu of previous versions, lists recently opened documents, and gives access to the application's control options, as shown in Fig. 2.8.

Fig. 2.8 The Office Button Menu for Access 2007

You click the **Office Button** to: **Open** a new or existing document (or database), **Save** the current one, **Save As** with another name or format, **Print** the current document or send it as an **E-mail**, and other commands such as **Manage**, **Publish** and **Close Database**.

Fig. 2.9 The Print Sub-Menu

Clicking the **Print** button opens a sub-menu, as shown here, giving easy access to your printer controls.

To change an application's settings in previous Office versions you clicked **Options** on the **Tools** menu. Now, all these settings are part of Access Options, which you open by clicking the **Access Options** button on the bottom of the Office Button menu, shown in Fig. 2.8 on the previous page. The Access Options box is opened, shown in Fig. 2.10 below.

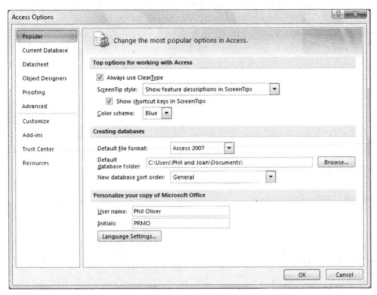

Fig. 2.10 The Access Options Dialogue Box

This dialogue box lets you change any of Access's settings and defaults. We recommend that you have a good look at the options available, although many may not mean much to you at the moment!

The Mini Toolbar

Some commands are so useful that you want to have them immediately available whatever you are doing. For these, Access 2007 shows a 'hovering' Mini Toolbar over your work when they are available.

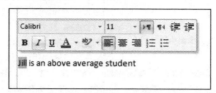

Fig. 2.11 A Mini Toolbar of Access Formatting Commands

In the example above, we were adding notes to a form in an Access 2007 database and wanted to quickly format some text. We selected it by dragging the mouse pointer and then pointed at the selection. A faded Mini toolbar appeared, which when pointed to became solid, as shown in Fig. 2.11. This offered a range of formatting options without having to go to any of the tabs on the Ribbon.

A Mini Toolbar will stay active for a selection until you click the document outside the selection. It will then disappear.

Galleries

Galleries are at the heart of the redesigned 'Pick and Click' interface. They provide you with a set of clear visual results to choose from when you are working in a document.

By presenting a simple set of potential results, rather than a complex dialogue box with numerous options, Galleries simplify the process of producing good-looking work. As we have seen, dialogue boxes are still available if you want more control over an operation, but a simple Gallery choice will very often be enough.

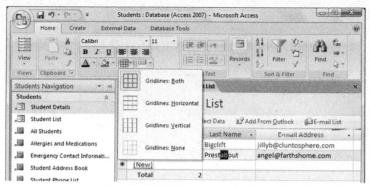

Fig. 2.12 A Gallery in Access 2007

As we show above, you can apply pre-set formats and styles from galleries in the Ribbon.

Quick Access Toolbar

Fig. 2.13 The Quick Access Toolbar

The Quick Access Toolbar is the small area to the upper left of the Ribbon, as shown in Fig. 2.13. It contains buttons for the things that you use over and over every day, such as **Save**, **Undo**, and **Repeat**, by default. The bar is always available, whatever you are doing in a program.

It is very easy to add your favourite commands to the Quick Access toolbar so they are available no matter which tab you are on. Here in Fig. 2.13 we have added a **Print Preview** command button. To do this we clicked the **Customize Quick Access Toolbar** button and selected **Print Preview** from the drop-down menu shown.

To add other command buttons to the bar you select the
More Commands option from the drop-down menu to open
the Access Options box as shown in Fig. 2.14.

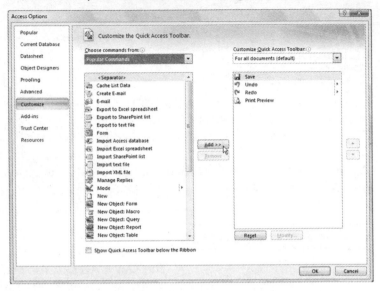

Fig. 2.14 Customising the Quick Access Toolbar

In the Customize tab, shown open above, you select any
commands in the left pane and click the **Add** button to place
them on the Quick Access toolbar. To remove them just do
the opposite.

You can control where the new buttons display by
selecting them in the right pane and clicking the up and down
arrows on the right-hand side. When you are happy click the
OK button.

3

The Access Environment

Starting Access

To start Access 2007 in Windows XP, use the *start*, **All Programs** command, select the **Microsoft Office** entry from the cascade menu, and click **Microsoft Office Access 2007** as shown in Fig. 3.1 below.

Fig. 3.1 Using the Start Menu in Windows XP

You can also double-click on an Access file in a Windows folder, in which case the database will be loaded into Access at the same time, and the Get Started page will not display.

Fig. 3.2 The Start Menu in Windows Vista

To start the program with Windows Vista use the **Start**, **All Programs** command, click the **Microsoft Office** entry, then click the **Microsoft Office Access 2007** option on the drop-down sub-menu, pointed to in Fig. 3.2.

Our favourite method is to create a shortcut on the Windows desktop. This is easily done by highlighting the Access entry in the Start menu, as shown on the previous page, dragging the pointer to the desktop with the right mouse button depressed, and selecting the **Create Shortcuts Here** option when the button is released. Double-clicking this shortcut 'icon', shown above, will open Access.

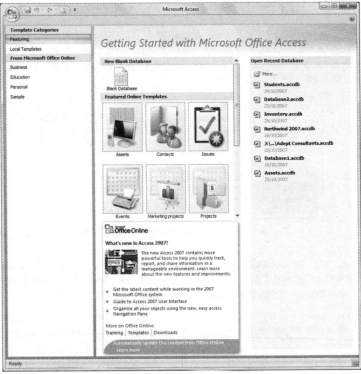

Fig. 3.3 The Access Get Started Page

Whichever method you use, the opening screen is similar to that of Publisher 2007 but very different from the other Office 2007 programs, as you can see in Fig. 3.3 above.

Access 2007 uses the new Office 2007 interface, but does not show the Ribbon until a database is actually open.

The centre pane of the Get Started window offers you a range of Templates to use, some installed on your computer, and some available for you to download from Microsoft Office Online. You have to have a legal version of Office 2007 to do this, though.

Clicking the **Template Categories** options in the left pane will open new choices in the centre pane. We had about 30 Template options in total. Templates are pre-built databases that you can open and use right away. When you select a template, Access 2007 shows you more about it in the pane on the right side of the Getting Started page, as shown here in Fig. 3.4. Here you can give the database a different name and either **Create**, or **Download** it.

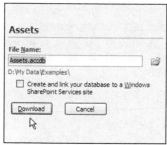

Fig. 3.4 Creating the Assets Database

You can also create a new blank database on this page by clicking the **Blank Database** button shown here.

If you have worked with any databases in Access 2007 they will be listed as links in the right-hand pane. Clicking one of these will reopen it for you.

At the bottom of the middle pane are a series of links to Microsoft Office Online features. These are well worth exploring when you have a few spare moments, and now is as good a time as ever!

Using a Database Template

As we have seen, Access provides a range of templates that you can use to speed up the database creation process. A template is a ready-to-use database containing all the tables, queries, forms, and reports needed to perform a specific task. There are templates for tracking 'issues', managing contacts, recording expenses, to name but a few. These can be used as they are, or you can customise them.

If one of these templates fits your needs, using it is usually the fastest way to get a database started. As an example we downloaded the Assets template from the Getting Started page, as shown in Fig. 3.5, and we show some of its features below.

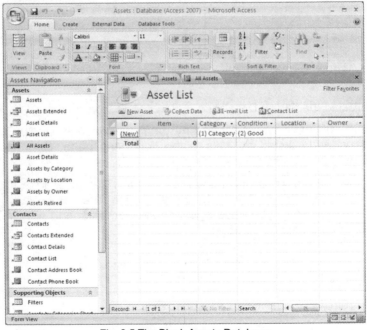

Fig. 3.5 The Blank Assets Database

It's worth having a good look at these templates, but they may be easier to use after reading a few more pages.

Parts of the Access Screen

Before we start designing a database, we will take a look at an Access 2007 opening screen. In Fig. 3.6, we show what displays if you select **New Blank Database** on the Getting Started page, which you can open at any time by clicking **New** from the **Office Button** menu.

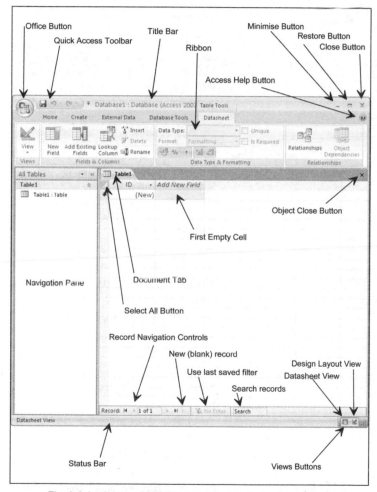

Fig. 3.6 An Access 2007 Starting Window in Datasheet View

The layout, as shown, is in a window, but if you click on the **Restore** button, you can make Access take up the full screen area available.

The Access window in our case displays an empty and untitled database (Database1). Access follows the usual Windows and Office 2007 conventions and if you are familiar with these you can skip some of this section.

Area	*Function*
Office Button	Located in the upper-left corner of the program window. This button replaces the File menu of previous versions, lists recently opened documents, and gives access to the application's control options.
Quick Access Toolbar	Located to the right of the Office button, it contains buttons that are always available for your most common commands, such as Save, Undo, and Repeat, by default.
Title Bar	The bar at the top of a window which displays the application name and the name of the current document or database.
Minimise Button	When clicked, this button minimises the application to an icon on the Windows Taskbar.
Restore Button	When clicked, this button restores the active window to the position and size that was occupied before it was maximised.
	The restore button is then replaced by a Maximise button, as shown here,

	which is used to set the window to full screen size.
Close button	The extreme top right button that you click to close a window.
Ribbon	The traditional menus and toolbars have been replaced by the Ribbon – a new device that presents commands organised into a set of tabs. Each tab has several Groups that show related Command items together.
Gallery	A control that displays a choice visually so that you can see the results that you will get.
Scroll Bars	The areas on the screen that contain scroll boxes in vertical and horizontal bars. Clicking on these bars allows you to control the part of a document which is visible on the screen.
Scroll Arrows	The arrowheads at each end of each scroll bar which you can click to scroll the screen up and down one line, or left and right 10% of the screen, at a time.
Insertion Point	The pointer used to indicate where text will be inserted.
Views Buttons	Clicking these buttons changes screen views quickly.
Status Bar	The bottom line of a database window that displays status information.

Navigation Pane

In Access 2007 the Database window used by earlier versions has been replaced by a new Navigation Pane.

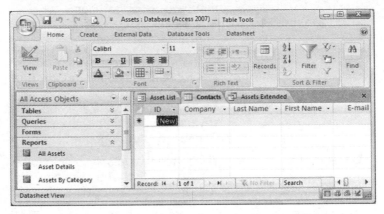

Fig. 3.7 Navigation Pane Controls and Document Tabs

When you open a new or existing database, its objects, such as tables, forms, reports, queries and macros, are listed in the Navigation Pane on the left of the Access window. Double-clicking an object in the Navigation Pane opens it in the right-hand pane, as shown in Fig. 3.7 above.

To open the Navigation Pane, if it is closed, click the **Shutter Bar Open/Close Button** » « on the pane title bar, or press **F11**. Both of these work in reverse as well to close the Pane. To choose what you see in the Navigation Pane, click the Menu button ▼ at the top of the pane and choose from the opened list.

Document Tabs

Access 2007 provides a new way to work with the tables, forms, reports, and other objects in a database. Instead of opening each object in a separate window, by default Access now places all opened objects in the right-hand pane and separates them with tabs. To move between the open objects you just click their tabs.

The Ribbon

Once you have opened a database in Access 2007 the Ribbon is the first major change you will notice. It replaces the older menu bar and toolbars that you are probably well used to. See page 25 for a general description of the Ribbon components and how to use them.

Access's Ribbon has four fixed tabs, each one with the most used controls grouped on it for the main program actions .

Fig. 3.8 The Home Tab of the Access 2007 Ribbon

A quick look at the **Home** tab, (Fig. 3.8 above), shows that it contains groups for the more common worksheet activities, such as, changing database Views, the Clipboard Cut and Paste commands, setting Font characteristics and alignment, applying Rich Text formatting to a memo field, working with Records, Sorting and Filtering records and Finding records.

Clicking a new tab opens a new series of groups, each with its relevant command buttons, as shown next.

Fig. 3.9 The Create Tab of the Access 2007 Ribbon

Under the **Create** tab, are groupings to enable you to create a new blank table, a new table using a table template, a list on a SharePoint site and a table in the current database that links to the newly created list, a new blank table in Design view, new forms based on the active table or query, a new pivot table or chart, a new report based on the active table or query, a new query, macro, module, or class module.

Fig. 3.10 The External Data Tab of the Access 2007 Ribbon

The **External Data** tab groups controls for you to Import or Link to external data, to Export data, to Collect and update data via e-mail, work with offline SharePoint lists, create Saved Imports and saved exports, and to move some or all parts of a database to a new or existing SharePoint site.

Fig. 3.11 The Database Tools Tab of the Access 2007 Ribbon

This tab lets you launch the Visual Basic editor or run a Macro, create and view table Relationships, Show/hide Object Dependencies, Analyse performance, Move Data to other databases, and run Database Tools.

The Status Bar

This is located at the bottom of the Access window and is used to display such things as status messages, property hints and progress indicators. To the right of the status bar are **Views** switching buttons and with some views a **Zoom Slider** control.

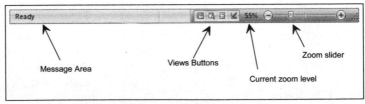

Fig. 3.12 The Access 2007 Status Bar

In Fig. 3.12 we were looking at an Access generated report in the Print Preview view.

You can control what appears on the **Status Bar** by right-clicking it and making selections in the Customize Status Box

Access Screen Views

Fig. 3.13

Access 2007 provides eight main display views, as described below. You control these viewing options, either from the **Status Bar**, or from the **Home**, **Views**, **View** button on the Ribbon, as shown in Fig. 3.13. What views are available here will depend on what database object is currently active. In our example a report is open in **Layout View**, and clicking the **View** button itself will change to **Report View**, as can be seen from the icon on the button. To open another view you select from the drop-down menu opened by clicking the down arrow ▼ below the **View** button.

The main view options have the following effect, and can also be accessed by clicking the **Views** buttons on the **Status Bar** at the bottom of the Access window (see Fig. 3.12).

Datasheet View

A view that displays data from a table, form, query, view, or stored procedure in a row-and-column format. In Datasheet view, you can edit fields, add and delete data, and search for data. You can also modify and add fields to a table in Datasheet view.

Design View

A view available for the following database objects; tables, queries, forms, reports, and macros.

In Design view, you can create new database objects and modify the design of existing objects.

Layout View

A view new to Access 2007 in which you can make design changes to forms and reports while using existing live data.

Report View

Another view new to Access 2007 which lets you browse an accurate rendering of a report without having to use Print Preview.

Print Preview

This shows what your print output will look like, and how much of your document will fit on the selected page size. The Print Preview window has its own Ribbon.

SQL View

SQL

An object tab that displays the SQL (Structured Query Language) statement for the current query.

When you create a query in Design view, Access constructs the SQL equivalent in SQL view.

PivotTable View

A view that summarises and analyses data in a datasheet or form. You can use different levels of detail or organise data by dragging the fields and items or by showing and hiding items in the drop-down lists for the fields.

PivotChart View

A view that shows a graphical analysis of data in a datasheet or form.

Access 2007 Options

You can, to a certain extent, control how Access looks and behaves by setting its options. You do this by clicking the **Office Button** (see page 30) followed by the **Access Options** command button . This opens the Access Options dialogue box shown in Fig. 3.14 below.

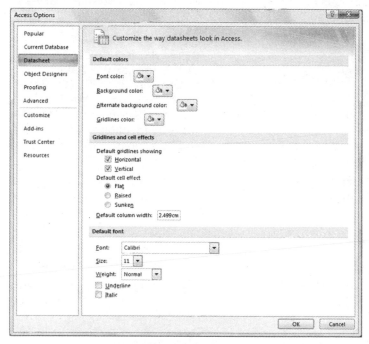

Fig. 3.14 The Access Options Dialogue Box

As can be seen, this box has ten tabbed sheets which give you control of most of the program's settings. A few minutes spent here will help you understand the workings of Access 2007.

Saving Your Work

When you first create a database in Access, either from a template or from scratch, you have to give it a file name and decide where on your hard disc it should be placed. From then on, the only time you have to manually save your work is if you make any changes to the design of any of the database objects. The data itself is saved automatically as it is entered.

Fig. 3.15 A Save As Box

The quickest way to save a document to disc is to click the **Save** button on the Quick Access toolbar. If an object is not saved, a Save As box will open for you to name the object. In Fig. 3.15 we have been asked to save a new table in our new database with the default name of **Table1**.

The usual way however is from the **Office Button** menu, shown in Fig. 3.16 below, which gives you more control of the saving operation.

Fig. 3.16 Saving Operations from the Office Button

- **Save** is used for an exiting database when you want to keep the existing filename. If any objects are not named you will be prompted to name them.

- **Save As** (selected above) is used when you want to save your database with a different name or file format, or in a different location.

Using the **Save As** command and selecting **Access 2007 Database** as the format, opens the dialogue box shown in Fig. 3.17 (for Windows Vista).

Note that a suggested name is placed and highlighted in the **File name** field box, with the program waiting for you to over-type a new name. Filenames must have less than 255 characters and cannot include any of the following keyboard characters: /, \, >, <, *, ?, ", |, :, or ;. Access 2007 adds the new file extension **.accdb** automatically and uses it to identify it as a 2007 database.

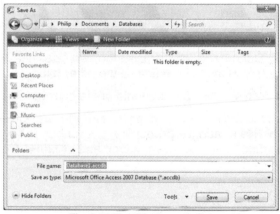

Fig. 3.17 The File Save As Box

You can select a different drive or folder in which to save your work by clicking **Folders** in the left pane and selecting from the hierarchical tree that opens. To create a new folder use the **New Folder** button. We used this facility to create a folder called **Databases** within the **Documents** folder (**My Documents** folder in Windows XP) and clicked the **Save** button to accept the default name.

Vista Folder Features

In Vista, most folders and file-related dialogue boxes have the following features:

Back and Forward buttons ⊙⊙▾ – Used to navigate to other folders you have already opened.

Address bar ⟨ ▸ Computer ▸ OS (C:) ▸ Users ▸ Phil ▸   ▾ ⁴⁷⟩ – Used to navigate to a different folder without closing the current folder window.

Search box ⟨Search   ⌕⟩ – Type a word or phrase in this, to look for a file or sub-folder stored in the current folder.

Toolbar ⟨ Organize ▾ Views ▾ New Folder ⟩ – Click buttons to perform common tasks, such as organising your files and folders, setting different views of them and creating a new folder. What buttons are actually on the toolbar depends on the action you are carrying out.

Navigation pane – Lets you change the view to other folders. The **Favorite Links** section makes it easy to open the more common locations on your computer, such as Pictures, Documents or the Desktop, whereas the **Folders** section lets you move between all the other folder locations.

File list – This shows the contents of the current folder.

Tags – Depending on the type of file you are saving, you might be able to add file properties (like author or key words) to act as tags. Later, you can search and organise files using these property tags.

Selecting File Location

You can select where Access automatically looks for your database files when you first choose to open or save a document, by clicking the **Office Button** ⊙, selecting the **Access Options** command and clicking the Popular tab of the displayed Access Options dialogue box, (Fig. 2.10 on page 31), and modifying the location of the **Default database folder**.

Microsoft suggests that you store documents, worksheets, presentations, databases, and other files you are currently working on, in the **Documents** folder (Vista), or in **My Documents** (Windows XP). These are easily accessed from the Desktop with the **Start** menu. This, of course, is a matter of preference, so we leave it to you to decide. We prefer to create sub-folders within **Documents** to group our files in.

While any of the file opening, saving and location dialogue boxes are open you can use them to generally manage your files and folders. You do this by right-clicking on the name of a file or folder you want to manipulate. A context sensitive menu is opened like ours in Fig. 3.18.

Fig. 3.18 A Context Menu

All of these options may not be available on your system, but the common ones of Open, New, Cut, Copy, Create Shortcut, Delete, Rename and Properties should be there.

Closing a Database

There are several ways to close an Access database. Once you have saved any changed objects you can click the window close [X] button. This will close Access 2007 as well. If you only want to close the active database click the **Office Button** and use the **Close Database** command, shown in Fig. 3.16.

Opening a Database

You can use the Open dialogue box in Access, shown in Fig. 3.19 on the next page, to open a database wherever it is located. This is opened by clicking the **Open** button on the **Office Button** menu, shown in Fig. 2.8, or with the **Ctrl+O** keystroke shortcut. Appendix A has a listing of the keyboard shortcuts that are available to you in Access.

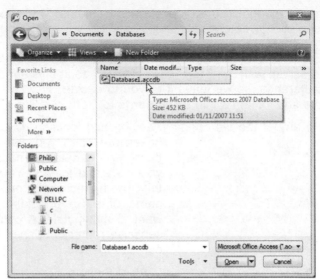

Fig. 3.19 The File Open Box

For example, you can open a database hidden on your computer's hard disc, or on a network drive that you have a connection to. To locate another drive and folder on your computer, click the **Computer** item in the Navigation pane, or click on items in the Address bar (see page 50). To locate a database stored on your network, click the **Folders** item in the Navigation pane, and then on **Network**. This opens a hierarchical list of available network locations, as shown above in Fig. 3.19. Once you have found your database, select its filename and click the **Open** button on the dialogue box.

The last few databases you worked on are also listed in the **Office Button** menu, as shown in Fig. 2.8 (page 30). Selecting one of these will quickly reopen that file.

If there are no past files displayed and you think there should be, open the Access Options dialogue box shown in Fig. 3.14, in the **Display** section of the Advanced tab sheet. Select a number against the **Show this number of Recent Documents** option and press **OK**. You can choose to have up to the last five databases listed.

4

Creating our Database

As an example, we will step through the process of creating a fairly simplistic databa[se] to demonstrate how it can be [used].

The database we are g[oing to create will hold] details which the small firm Adept Consultants keep on their business. One table will hold the details of their clients, another will hold details of orders received, while yet another will hold invoice details. We suggest you work your way through this example to get to grips with Access 2007.

Creating a Blank Database

Before we start the process we have to create a blank database. As we saw earlier (see page 37) we do this on the Getting Started page by clicking **Blank Database** in the **New Blank Database** section.

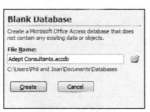

Blank Database

Create a Microsoft Office Access database that does not contain any existing data or objects.

File Name:

Adept Consultants.accdb

C:\Users\Phil and Joan\Documents\Databases

[Create] [Cancel]

Fig. 4.1 Creating a Blank Database

In the Blank Database pane, type a suitable name for the database in the **File Name** box, we will use 'Adept Consultants' for our example. To change the location of the file from the default, click the **Browse** button and look for a location to put your database, we used the **Databases** folder we had already created in **Documents**.

When you click the **Create** button, Access creates the database with an empty table (named Table1) open in Datasheet View. The cursor is placed in the first empty cell in the Add New Field column, as shown next in Fig. 4.2.

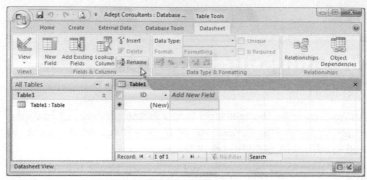

Fig. 4.2 The Starting Blank Database

You can immediately add a field by typing some information in the Add New Field column, but please don't do that yet, or you will be in danger of incrementing the ID field every time you add a new field. As the ID field will be our primary key field we only want it to increment for new rows.

To stop this happening rename the field by clicking the **Datasheet**, **Fields & Columns**, **Rename** button pointed to above and type 'Company' into the selected cell space, as shown in Fig. 4.3 below.

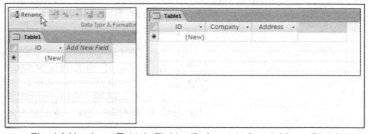

Fig. 4.3 Naming a Table's Fields. (Before – Left and After – Right)

Now would be a good time to enter all the field names. Just type the name in the field header and press **Enter** to move to the next one, as we show on the right above. For our example get the field names from our printout of the Customers table shown later in Fig. 4.6.

Creating a Table

In a table, you store the information items you want to track in fields, or columns. In our example we have created fields for names, addresses and phone numbers, among others. If you need to report, sort, search or calculate on an item of information, you should put it in a field of its own.

Every field has a Name that uniquely identifies it within the table. A field also has a data type chosen to match the information to be stored. The data type determines the values that can be stored and the operations that can be performed on them. Every field also has a group of settings, or properties, that define how the field looks and behaves. Appendix B gives details of Access' data types and field properties.

Entering information in Datasheet View is very similar to working in an Excel worksheet. The table structure is created while you enter data. When you add a new column to the table, a new field is defined, and Access automatically sets a data type, based on the first data you enter.

Renaming a Table

Fig. 4.4 Renaming a Table

To rename the table, from 'Table1', right-click its tab and select **Save** from the context menu. Then type the new name, 'Customers' in our case, into the **Save As** box that opens.

Fig. 4.5 The Navigation Pane

If you look at the Navigation Pane, you will see that this has changed, as shown in Fig. 4.5. The renamed table has been put inside a new Customers group. Any new objects we create from it will also be placed here.

If you haven't done so already, enter all the data from Fig. 4.6 on the next page, into the table. It only takes a few minutes and will help you master the Datasheet View.

Customers			
CustomerID ▾	Company ▾	Address ▾	Town ▾
1	VORTEX Co. Ltd	Windy House	St. Austell
2	AVON Construction	Riverside House	Stratford on Avon
3	BARROWS Associates	Barrows House	Bodmin
4	STONEAGE Ltd	Data House	Salisbury
5	PARKWAY Gravel	Aggregate House	Bristol
6	WESTWOOD Ltd	Weight House	Plymouth
7	GLOWORM Ltd	Light House	Brighton
8	SILVERSMITH Co	Radiation House	Exeter
9	WORMGLAZE Ltd	Glass House	Winchester
10	EALING Engines Design	Engine House	Taunton
11	HIRE Service Equipment	Network House	Bath
12	EUROBASE Co. Ltd	Control House	Penzance
*	(New)		

County ▾	Post Code ▾	Contact ▾	Phone ▾	Fax ▾
Cornwall	TR18 1FX	Brian Storm	01776 223344	01776 224466
Warwickshire	AV15 2QW	John Waters	01657 113355	01657 221133
Cornwall	PL22 1XE	Mandy Brown	01554 664422	01554 663311
Wiltshire	SB44 1BN	Mike Irons	01765 234567	01765 232332
Avon	BS55 2ZX	James Stone	01534 987654	01534 984567
Devon	PL22 1AA	Mary Slim	01234 667755	01234 669988
Sussex	BR87 4DD	Peter Summer	01432 746523	01432 742266
Devon	EX28 1PL	Adam Smith	01336 997755	01336 996644
Hampshire	WN23 5TR	Richard Glazer	01123 654321	01123 651234
Somerset	TN17 3RT	Trevor Miles	01336 010107	01336 010109
Avon	BA76 3WE	Nicole Webb	01875 558822	01875 552288
Cornwall	TR15 8LK	Sarah Star	01736 098765	01736 098567

Fig. 4.6 The Customers Table (Split into two parts)

To change the width of a field, place the cursor on the column separator until the cursor changes to the vertical split arrow, then drag the column separator to the right or left, to increase or decrease the width of the field.

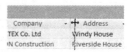

Fig. 4.7 Changing Field Width

Using Table Templates

In Access 2007 you can use table and field templates to easily create standardised pre-formed tables and fields. The following table templates are available to you:

Contacts   Creates a table for managing business contact information, including e-mail addresses, Web page URLs, and attachments, such as a service contract and a photo.

Tasks   Creates a table for tracking tasks, which includes a field for attachments.

Issues   Creates a table for tracking issues, including a field for attachments and an append-only Memo field that keeps a history of old field values.

Events   Creates a table for managing events, which includes a rich text Memo field and a field for attachments.

Assets   Creates a table for managing business assets, which includes two currency fields so that you can track asset depreciation.

To create a new table using a table template, open the database, click the **Create**, **Tables**, **Table Templates** button and then select one of the available templates from the list as shown here in Fig. 4.8.

A new table is placed in your database. If you are lucky, you can use it straight away. If not, you will have to edit its fields using some of the techniques described later.

Fig. 4.8 The Available Table Templates

Using Field Templates

You can also add fields to an existing table using predefined field templates. You do this in Datasheet View by clicking the **Datasheet**, **Fields & Columns**, **New Field** button to open the Field Templates pane as shown in Fig. 4.9 below.

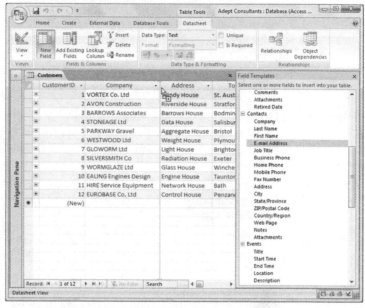

Fig. 4.9 Adding a Field Template to a Table

Then you simply select one or more fields in the Field Templates pane and drag them to the table. When the insertion line appears where you want to position the field (as shown above), just drop the field in place.

When suitable options are available in the Fields Template pane this makes a very easy way of adding fields to your tables. Otherwise you will have to create them yourself.

Design View

Clicking the **Design View** button, shown here, on the bottom right of the Access status bar, first asks you to save any unsaved objects, and then opens the current table in Design View, as shown below.

Fig. 4.10 The Customers Table in Design View

In Design View you can change the data type and properties of the fields in a table and give each one a description which is then displayed when that field is used in the database.

As each **Field Name** is highlighted, the **Field Properties** pane at the bottom of the window is shown. If you were using this Design View to rename fields, then you should also edit the name appearing against the Caption property, or remove it altogether.

Clicking the cursor in the Data Type cell of the CustomerID field and then clicking the down-arrow button which appears displays a drop-down list of the data types available, as shown here in Fig. 4.11 and explained below.

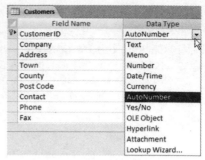

Fig. 4.11 List of Data Types

Data Types and Field Properties

The data type of an Access field controls what kind of data can be stored in it. For instance, a field with the **Text** data type can store data that consists of either text or numerical characters, but a field with the **Number** data type can store only numerical data.

When you create a field by entering data in Datasheet View, Access automatically assigns a data type to the field based on the data you enter. But when you create a new field in Design View you specify the field's data type and, optionally, its other properties.

Data Types

There are ten different data types in Access 2007, as listed below. Appendix B gives more details about the data types and their properties.

Attachment	New to Access 2007, this data type can store files, such as digital photos or Word documents. Multiple files can be attached per record.
AutoNumber	This data type automatically generates a unique number for each record.
Currency	For the storage of monetary values.

Date/Time	For the storage of dates and times.
Hyperlink	Used for hyperlinks, such as e-mail addresses or Web pages.
Memo	For the storage of long blocks of text that can use text formatting. A typical use of a Memo field would be a detailed description of something.
Number	For the storage of numeric values, such as dimensions and distances, but not currency which has its own data type.
OLE Object	For the storage of OLE objects (**O**bject **L**inking and **E**mbedding). These can be linked or embedded in a field, form, or report.
Text	For the storage of short, alphanumeric values, such as a names or addresses.
Yes/No	For the storage of Boolean values.

As shown in Fig. 4.9, you can also set a field's data type to **Lookup Wizard**. This starts the Lookup Wizard, which helps you create a field that uses a combo box to look up a value in another table, query or list of values.

Field Properties

After you create a field and set its data type, you can set additional field properties. For example, you can control the size of a Text field by setting its Field Size property.

For Number and Currency fields, the Field Size property is particularly important, because it determines the range of field values. For example, a one-bit Number field can store only integers ranging from 0 to 255.

The Field Size property also determines how much disc space each Number field value requires. Depending on the field size, the number can take up exactly 1, 2, 4, 8, 12, or 16 bytes.

Sorting a Database Table

To sort a database table, place the cursor in the required field and click the **Table Tools**, **Sort & Filter** buttons. **Ascending** 斜 for an A to Z sort or **Descending** 斜 for a Z to A sort. To cancel sorting click the **Clear All Sorts** 斜 button. You can also click the **Sort and Filter** button · at the top of a field and select from the menu, as shown below.

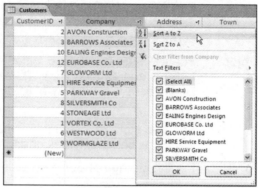

Fig. 4.12 Sorting a Table in Datasheet View

Applying a Filter to a Sort

If you want to sort and display only records that fit selected criteria, use the **Table Tools**, **Sort & Filter**, **Filter** button, which opens the same Sort and Filter box, shown above and in Fig. 4.13 on the next page.

The upper three options are for sorting, with the filter controls below them. All the entries in the field have a check box option. To filter out specific records you can check them and press **OK**.

Ticking the **Select All** option either selects all the check boxes or clears them. The **Text Filters** option opens a menu of filter criteria for you to select. In our example, we chose to view the records within the Customer field that start with 'W' as shown in the Custom Filter box open in Fig. 4.13.

Fig. 4.13 Applying a Table Filter

When we clicked the **OK** button the Customers table displayed with only two entries, as seen in Fig. 4.14 below.

Fig. 4.14 Filtering a Table in Datasheet View

To revert to the display of all the records, click the **Table Tools**, **Sort & Filter**, **Remove Filter** button , which 'lights up' whenever a filter action is active.

Using a Database Form

With a table active, if you click the **Create**, **Forms**, **Form** button, Access will automatically create a form for you to view the table data one record at a time. The created form for the Customers table is shown in Fig. 4.15 on the next page. Before the Form is created you will be asked to save the Customers table, as it depends on it.

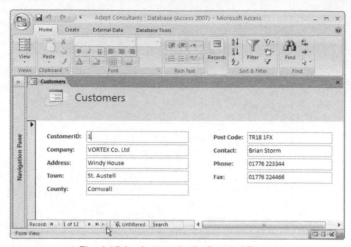

Fig. 4.15 An Automatically Created Form

Forms can be used to enter, change or view data and are mainly used to improve the way in which data is displayed on the screen. They can also be used to sort records in a database table in descending or ascending order of a selected field.

When you attempt to close a new Form, you will be asked if you want to save it. An Access database can have lots of different forms, each designed with a different purpose in mind. Saved forms are displayed in the Navigation Pane and can be opened by double-clicking on their entry there. Later on we will discuss Form design in a little more detail, including their customisation.

You use the navigation controls, shown in Fig. 4.16 below, at the bottom left of a form, to move through the table data.

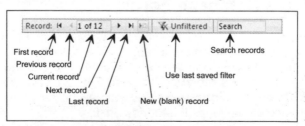

Fig. 4.16 The Record Control Bar

Selecting Data

As with most Windows programs, before you can carry out an action on part of a database, you must first select it. Selected data is highlighted as shown below.

Selecting Fields

Fig. 4.17 Selecting a Table Field

A field is a vertical column in a database table. To select it, move the mouse over the field name at the top of the column, and when the pointer changes to a ↓ shape, simply click to select the one field, or drag the pointer across several columns and release it to select those fields.

Selecting Records

A record, on the other hand, is a horizontal row in a database table. To select it, move the mouse into the area to the left of the record and when the pointer changes to a → shape, simply click to select the one record, or drag the pointer up or down across several rows and release it to select those records.

Fig. 4.18 Selecting Table Records

Selecting Cells

To select a cell, move the mouse over the left edge of the cell and the pointer will change to a ⇧ shape. Simply click this pointer to select the cell, or drag it across the required cells and release it to select more than one.

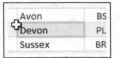

Fig. 4.19
Selecting a Cell

Selecting Data in a Cell

Fig. 4.20
Selecting Data

To select data actually inside a cell, position the I-beam pointer Ⅰ in the data, left-click and drag the pointer to highlight the required data, as shown here in Fig. 4.20.

To cancel any selection, you just click the mouse outside the selected area.

Zooming into a Cell

If you need to view or edit the contents of a cell that are not visible in a table because the column width is too narrow, you can open a zoom window on the cell. To do this, click the cell and press the **Shift+F2** key combination.

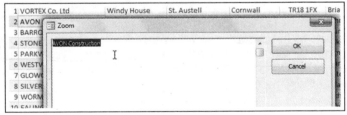

Fig. 4.21 Zooming in to the Contents of a Cell

Once the Zoom dialogue box opens, you can view the whole content of the cell. You can edit and change the font of the cell contents in this box as well, which makes life far easier as you can see what you are doing. When you have finished with the cell, click the **OK** button to close the Zoom box. Any changes you have made will be automatically saved for you.

Working with Data

Adding Records to a Table

Whether you are in Datasheet or Form View, to add a record, click the **New (blank) record** button, shown in Fig. 4.16.

In Datasheet View, the cursor jumps to the first empty record in the table (the one with the asterisk in the box to the left of the first field). When in Form View, Access displays an empty form which can be used to add a new record.

Finding Records in a Table

Whether you are in Datasheet or Form View, to find a record, type the text to search for in the Search box, shown in Fig 4.16. As you enter letters search results will be offered. Carry on typing until you find the result you want.

For more refined searches, use the **Table Tools**, **Find**, **Find** button to open the Find and Replace box, shown below. In the **Look In** box you can choose to search the currently selected field, or the whole table.

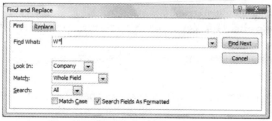

Fig. 4.22 The Find and Replace Box

To find all the Company records starting with **W**, we typed **W*** in the **Find What** box. Clicking the **Find Next** button, highlighted the first record 'WESTWOOD Ltd'. Clicking the **Find Next** button again, highlighted the next record matching our criteria, 'WORMGLAZE Ltd'.

Deleting Records from a Table

To delete a record when in Datasheet View, right-click in the box to the left of the record to highlight, or select, the entire record, as shown below, and choose the **Delete Record** option from the context menu that opens.

	8 SILVERSMITH Co	Radiation House	Exeter
→	9 WORMGLAZE Ltd	Glass House	Winchester
	10 EALING Engines Design	Engine House	Taunton

Fig. 4.23 Selecting a Record

Deleting Records from a Form

Fig. 4.24

To delete a record when in Form View, first display the record you want to delete, then right-click in the vertical bar on the left of the form to select the whole record, and choose **Cut** from the context menu, as shown here.

You can also use the **Home**, **Records**, **Delete** button. If the whole record is selected it will delete the record. If not it will delete the data in the active cell. If the whole record is selected you can also just press the **Del** key. All the methods give you a chance to back out with a warning box.

Fig. 4.25 A Strong Warning

As your database gets more complex you will link tables together and you will then find that Access 2007 won't let you delete any records that have related records in other tables, as shown in Fig. 4.26.

Fig. 4.26 A Denial Message Box

The Office Clipboard

As is usual with Windows applications, the cutting and copying of objects and text places them on the clipboard. Microsoft Office 2007 retains the extra clipboard in which you can store up to 24 cut or copied items until they are needed. You can paste any of these stored items into Access or another Office application. Each item is displayed as a thumbnail on the Clipboard Task Pane as shown in Fig. 4.27 below.

The Clipboard Task Pane

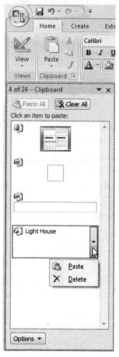

Fig. 4.27 The Clipboard Task Pane

If the Clipboard Task Pane does not open automatically you can open it by clicking the **Home**, **Clipboard** dialogue box launcher.

The **Clipboard** Task Pane in Fig. 4.27, shows several text items and graphics. Clicking on a text item on the Clipboard, pastes that item at the cursor position within an Access Form or Datasheet. If you click the down arrow to the right of a selected item in the Clipboard list, a menu opens as shown here. Selecting **Paste** will place the text in the current cursor location in the database. Selecting **Delete** will remove the item from the list.

When the Office Clipboard Task Pane is active the icon is added to the Notification Area at the right end of the Windows Taskbar. Moving the pointer over this icon will display the number of items held in the Clipboard, whatever Windows application you are currently using.

Manipulating Table Columns

Fig. 4.28
Shortcut Menu

Perhaps the easiest way to manipulate the columns of an Access table is to select the column, or columns, and use the menu that is opened by right-clicking the column, as shown here in Fig. 4.28.

This gives a range of rapid options that are available. You can sort the column, or field, in ascending or descending order, **Copy** the column contents to the clipboard, and then **Paste** them to an empty column, either in the same table, or in another one.

The other menu features are described in the next few sections.

Adjusting Column Widths

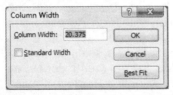

Fig. 4.29 Setting Column
Widths

Selecting **Column Width** from the above menu opens the small box shown here, which gives you three options. You can type an exact width in the **Column Width** text box, select **Standard Width** to force the Access default width of about one 'screen inch', or click **Best Fit**. The last option sets the column width so that both the heading and all field values are visible. Not much use if you have long text items in your fields, but excellent for simpler columns.

On page 56 we saw that an easy, if imprecise, way to change the width of a column was to drag the ✛ shaped pointer in the column selector at the top of a column. There is also a quick way to select the 'Best Fit' width for a column, by double-clicking this ✛ pointer on the right border of the column selector.

Hiding Fields

To reduce the data displayed on the screen you may find it useful to hide one or more columns, by first selecting them and then using the **Hide Columns** command from the right-click shortcut menu.

A hidden field is, of course, not deleted from the database, it is just made temporarily invisible. To unhide fields simply use the **Unhide Columns** context menu command.

Fig. 4.30 Hiding and Unhiding Table Columns

This command opens the dialogue box shown above. In this example we have hidden the Company field, to unhide it we would need to check its box in the **Column** list and click **Close**.

Freezing Fields

Fig. 4.31 A Frozen Column

The **Freeze Columns** menu option on the right-click shortcut menu moves selected columns to the left of a table and always displays them. In Fig. 4.31 the 'Company' field has been frozen.

You can only cancel this operation with the **Unfreeze All Columns** command. This, however, leaves the previously frozen columns still moved to the left of the table. As long as you have not saved the table with its columns frozen, you can close the table (without saving it) and re-open it in its original state. If you have saved the table, to return it to its original format you will have to move the fields back to where they 'started'.

Moving a Field

To move a field from its current position to a new position in a table, select the field you want to move, make sure it is not frozen, then click on the column selector so that the mouse pointer changes to that shown here, and drag the row to its new position.

Fig. 4.32 Moving a Field

Note that while you are dragging the field, a solid vertical bar shows where the field will be placed when the mouse button is released, as shown in Fig. 4.32 above.

Inserting, Renaming and Deleting Fields

To insert a field in a table in Datasheet View, select the field to the right of where you want it, right-click in the selection and choose **Insert Column** from the context menu, as shown in our composite Fig. 4.33 on the next page. Here we show the menu selections as well as the final result.

Select your new column, which is named Field 1, and then use the **Rename Column** menu command, type the new name and press **Enter**. It's as easy as that.

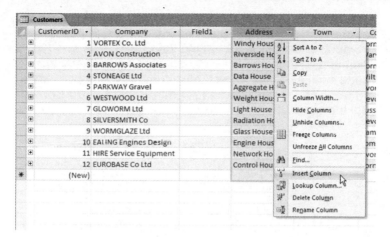

Fig. 4.33 Inserting a Column into a Table

To delete a field from a table, close any forms that might be open, load the table from the Navigation Pane, then select the field column by clicking its name. Right-click in the field and select **Delete Column** from the context menu.

You can also use the **Home**, **Records**, **Delete** button ✕ Delete ▾ and select **Delete Column**, or use the **Del** key. As before they all give you a similar warning before the deletion is carried out. Accepting **Yes** will action the deletion.

Adding a Lookup Column

Fig. 4.34 A Lookup Column

There are times with most databases when a particular field requires only one of a limited number of possible entries. A good example might be the title field for the details of a person. These could be Mr, Mrs, Miss, Ms, Dr, etc. In Access you can include this list in a Lookup Column, as we show here in Fig 4.34.

When a cell is opened in this field a down-arrow button appears which, when clicked, opens the list of possibilities for you to choose from. Anything that saves time and typing when adding data has to be good news! To open the Wizard to add such a column, select the column to the right of where you want it to be, right-click in it, and select **Lookup Column** from the shortcut menu.

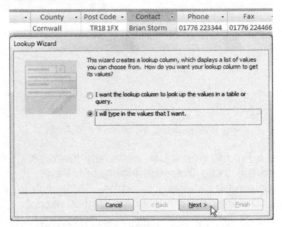

Fig. 4.35 The Lookup Wizard Opening Page

Opt to 'type in the values that I want' and click **Next** to go to the next Wizard box shown completed below. We will explore the other option in the next chapter.

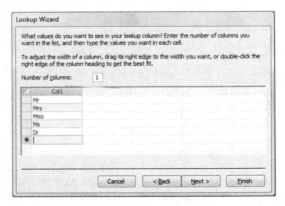

Fig. 4.36 Building a Lookup List

Make sure you select '1' as the **Number of columns** and then type the list entries one at a time. To move to the next cell press the **Tab** key. When you are happy with your list click the **Next** button and type in a suitable label for the field column. In our example 'Title' would be suitable, then click **Finish** to do just that.

Editing a Lookup List

Fig. 4.37 Editing List Items

If you need to make changes to a Lookup list, this is made very easy in Access 2007. Whenever you open the Lookup by selecting the cell and clicking the down-arrow button, a Mini Toolbar button  appears below the list, as shown earlier in Fig. 4.34.

Clicking this button opens the Edit List Items box shown here in Fig. 4.37. In this you can add, change or delete items from your Lookup list. You can also enter a **Default Value** which will be automatically selected when you add new records to the table. When your changes are complete clicking **OK** will action them.

You can also control a Lookup list in the Design View of a database table. In this view, click the **Data Type** cell of the field with the Lookup column and then select the Lookup tab, as shown in Fig. 4.38 on the next page. In the **Row Source** section of the **Field Properties** list you can see the values that will appear in the Lookup column.

To edit this list, click in it to select it and then click the 'dotted' **Build** button ⊡ to the right. This opens the Edit List Items box, shown above in Fig. 4.37, for you to make the changes you want.

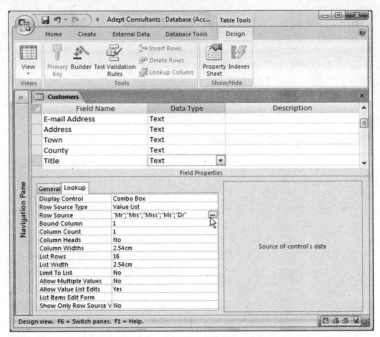

Fig. 4.38 Editing a Lookup List in Design View

Although the lookup list, or column, we have created here is quite useful, the most common type of lookup is one that displays values looked up from a related table or query in the database.

We will step through the procedure of doing this in the next chapter, when we create more tables in the database.

5

Relational Database Design

The Lookup Wizard

In order to be able to discuss relational databases, we will add an Orders table to our database by doing the following:

- Open the **Adept Consultants** database and click the **Create**, **Tables**, **Table** button ▦Table.

- Click the **Design View** button 📐 on the right end of the Status bar.

- Give the new table the name 'Orders'.

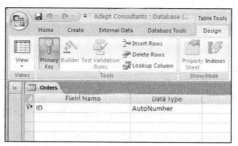

Fig. 5.1 Renaming the First Field in Design View

- Rename the ID field (the only one at the moment) 'OrdersID' and click the **Datasheet View** button ▦.

- We want the next field, CustomerID, to link to the Customers table and hold the value shown in the CustomerID field there, but to display the actual company name, to make it easier to work with. This is a 'Lookup'. First, click the **Datasheet**, **Fields & Columns**, **Add Existing Fields** button shown here, to open the Field List.

- In the Field List, double-click on the CustomerID entry, as shown in Fig. 5.2. This will open the Lookup Wizard we encountered in the last chapter, but will step through the Lookup procedure as if the **I want the lookup column to look up the values in a table or query box** had been selected. In our case the fields of the Customers table are offered, as shown in the left pane of Fig. 5.3.

Fig. 5.2 The Field List

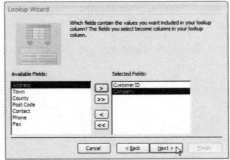

Fig. 5.3 Selecting Fields in the Lookup Wizard Window

- In the Wizard window shown in Fig. 5.3, move the fields CustomerID and Company to the right pane.

- Accept CustomerID Ascending as the sort parameters.

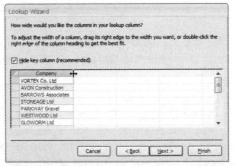

Fig. 5.4 Adjusting the Lookup Column Width

- Adjust the column width as in Fig. 5.4 and click **Next**.

- If asked, select CustomerID as the Primary Key, or unique identifier in the Customers table. Access uses primary key fields to associate data from multiple tables. A primary key must always have a unique value that does not change. By default, Access 2007 sets the primary key to the first field in a new table and gives it the AutoNumber data type.

- In the last Wizard window, select CustomerID as the label for the lookup column, click **Finish**, and change back to Design View, saving when asked.

Fig. 5.5 The Completed Table Layout in Design View

- To finish the table design, enter the last three field names as shown in Fig. 5.5 above, and set their **Data Types** the same as ours.

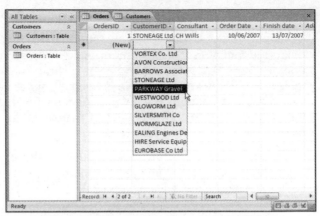

Fig. 5.6 The Lookup Working in Datasheet View

The information you need to enter in the Orders table is shown in Fig. 5.7 below. Note that the entries in the CustomerID field are not typed in, but selected from the lookup by clicking the down-arrow SILVERSMITH Co ▾, as shown in Fig. 5.6 above.

OrderID	CustomerID	Consultant	Order Date	Finish Date
1	STONEAGE Ltd	CH Wills	10/06/2007	13/07/2006
2	PARKWAY Gravel	AD Smith	15/06/2007	02/08/2007
3	WESTWOOD Ltd	WA Brown	16/07/2007	03/08/2007
4	GLOWORM Ltd	LS Stevens	28/07/2007	26/08/2007
5	SILVERSMITH Co	SF Adams	02/08/2007	18/08/2007
6	WORMGLAZE Ltd	CH Wills	05/08/2007	21/08/2007
7	EALING Engines Design	AD Smith	10/08/2007	17/10/2007
8	HIRE Service Equipment	WA Brown	12/08/2007	21/08/2007
9	EUROBASE Co Ltd	LS Stevens	18/08/2007	17/09/2007
10	AVON Construction	SF Adams	23/08/2007	24/09/2007
11	VORTEX Co. Ltd	AD Smith	01/09/2007	02/10/2007
12	AVON Construction	WA Brown	10/09/2007	09/10/2007
13	BARROWS Associates	SF Adams	26/09/2007	18/10/2007
14	SILVERSMITH Co	CH Wills	10/10/2007	22/10/2007
(New)				

Fig. 5.7 The Data for the Orders Table

Relationships

Information held in two or more tables of a database is normally related in some way. In our case, the two tables, Customers and Orders, are related by the CustomerID field.

To see our relationships, click the **Database Tools**, **Show/Hide**, **Relationships** command button. As the database contains relationships, the Relationships window appears. If the database did not contain any relationships and you are opening the Relationships window for the first time, the Show Table dialogue box appears.

Clicking the **Design**, **Relationships**, **All Relationships** button will display all of the defined relationships of your database.

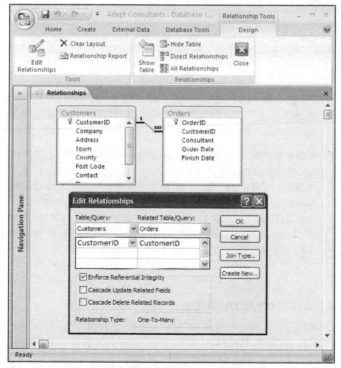

Fig. 5.8 The Relationships Window

In our case the relationship between our two tables is shown in the Relationships window displayed in Fig. 5.8. Note the relationship '1 customer to many (∞) orders' symbolism in the Relationships window. Clicking the **Edit Relationships** button opens the Edit Relationships dialogue box shown in Fig. 5.8. This is where you can set or change relationships between your database objects.

Note: Because Access is a relational database, data can be used in queries from more than one table at a time. As we have seen, if the database contains tables with related data, the relationships can be defined easily.

Usually, the matching fields have the same name, as in our example of Customers and Orders tables. In the Customers table, the CustomerID field is the primary key field and relates to the CustomerID field in the Orders table – there can be several orders in the Orders table from one customer in the Customers table.

The various types of relationships are as follows:

*   Inherited – for attaching tables from another Access database. The original relationships of the attached database can be used in the current database.

*   Referential – for enforcing relationships between records according to certain rules, when you add or delete records in related tables within the same database. You can only add records to a related table, if a matching record already exists in the primary table, and you cannot delete a record from the primary table if matching records exist in a related table.

Help on Relationships

For more help on relationships we suggest you look at the **Guide to Table Relationships** in the Access Help system, as shown in Fig. 5.9 on the next page.

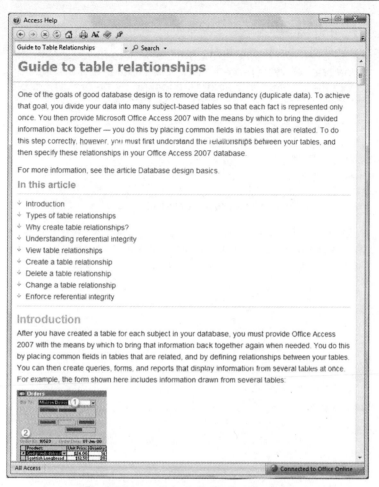

Fig. 5.9 Access Help on Table Relationships

 Probably the quickest way to find this page is to open the Help system either by pressing the **F1** function key, or clicking the **Microsoft Office Access Help** button shown here. Then type 'guide to table relationships' in the **Type words to search for** box, as shown above and in Fig. 1.17 on page 21. Clicking the **Search** button should show a link to the page.

Creating an Additional Table

As an exercise, create a third table, called 'Invoices', in the same way as we created the Orders table. Make sure you create the CustomerID field as a lookup as before. The table structure is shown in Fig. 5.10 in Design View.

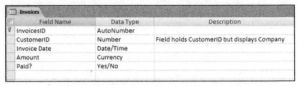

Field Name	Data Type	Description
▼ InvoicesID	AutoNumber	
CustomerID	Number	Field holds CustomerID but displays Company
Invoice Date	Date/Time	
Amount	Currency	
Paid?	Yes/No	

Fig. 5.10 The Invoices Table in Design View

Next, enter the data given below. Remember that the text shown under CustomerID is not typed in, but selected from the lookup by clicking the cell down-arrow SILVERSMITH Co ▼.

InvoicesID	CustomerID	Invoice Date	Amount	Paid?
1	STONEAGE Ltd	10/06/2007	£450.87	☑
2	PARKWAY Gravel	15/06/2007	£1,232.00	☐
3	WESTWOOD Ltd	16/07/2007	£543.90	☑
4	GLOWORM Ltd	28/07/2007	£876.00	☐
5	SILVERSMITH Co	02/08/2007	£986.00	☑
6	WORMGLAZE Ltd	05/08/2007	£326.00	☐
7	EALING Engines Design	10/08/2007	£478.98	☑
8	HIRE Service Equipment	12/08/2007	£1,689.60	☐
9	EUROBASE Co Ltd	18/08/2007	£1,053.00	☐
10	AVON Construction	23/08/2007	£1,385.00	☑
11	VORTEX Co. Ltd	01/09/2007	£1,400.00	☐
12	AVON Construction	10/09/2007	£1,200.00	☐
13	BARROWS Associates	26/09/2007	£345.00	☐
14	SILVERSMITH Co	10/10/2007	£657.50	☐
*	(New)			☐

Fig. 5.11 The Invoices Table in DataSheet View

The relationships between the three tables should be arranged as shown in Fig. 5.12 on the next page.

It is important that you complete this exercise, as it consolidates what we have done so far and, in any case, we will be using all three tables in what comes next. So go ahead and try it, the resultant database will be saved automatically under its original filename **Adept Consultants**.

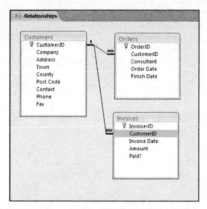

Fig. 5.12 The Relationships between Tables

Printing a Table View

Fig. 5.13 Print Menu Options

You can print a database table by, first clicking the **Office Button** , and then clicking the **Print** button to open the sub-menu shown here in Fig. 5.13.

Click the **Quick Print** option to print the table using the default printer and current settings, or use the **Print** option to open the Print dialogue box, shown in Fig. 5.14 on the next page, to control the print settings.

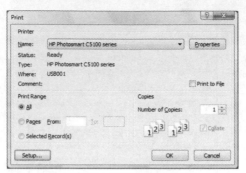

Fig. 5.14 The Print Dialogue Box

A better option, certainly to start with, is to preview the output on screen by clicking the **Print Preview** button.

However, printing directly from datasheet or form views, produces a predefined printout, the format of which you cannot control, apart from the margins and print orientation. For a better method of producing printed output, see the **Report Design** section in a later chapter.

6

Creating Queries

In Access you create a query so that you can ask questions about the data in your database tables. For example, we could find out whether we have more than one order from the same customer in our Adept Consultants database.

To do this, start Access, open **Adept Consultants**, and click the **Create**, **Other**, **Query Wizard** button, to open the Wizard.

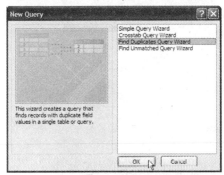

When you make the selection shown here and click **OK**, the Find Duplicates Query Wizard dialogue box opens, as shown in Fig. 6.2 below.

Fig. 6.1 Using the Find Duplicate Query Wizard

Fig. 6.2 Selecting a Table

Select the Orders table from the list and press the **Next** button. In the next dialogue box double-click **CustomerID** as the field you want to check for duplicate values, this will move it to the right pane (or you could use the ⊡ button), followed by the **Next** button.

Finally, select the additional fields you would like to see along with the duplicate values, by selecting from the next dialogue box, either one at a time or, if you decide to select all of them, as shown here, by clicking the ⊡⊡ button.

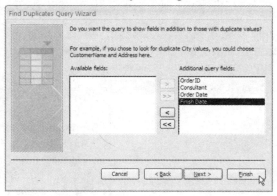

Fig. 6.3 Selecting Additional Fields for the Query

Clicking the **Finish** button ends the Wizard, which in our case displayed the results shown in Fig. 6.4.

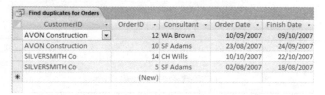

Fig. 6.4 The Select Query Results

Not very exciting in itself, but if the database held hundreds of records, that would be a different thing. When you close the query, you will be given the option to automatically save it. This is important as queries are often used to select the data for further actions. Once you have saved one, the next time it is used it will include any new added data.

Types of Queries

The query we have created so far, is known as a *Select Query*, which is the most common type of query. It is used to create subsets of data to answer specific questions, or to supply data to other database objects. With Access you can also create and use other types of queries, as follows:

- **Crosstab query** – used to present data with row and column headings, just like a spreadsheet. It can be used to summarise large amounts of data in a more readable form.

- **Action query** – used to make changes to many records in one operation. For example, you might like to remove from a given table all records that meet certain criteria, make a new table, or append records to a table. These must be treated with care!

- **Union query** – used to match fields from tables.

- **Pass-through query** – used to pass commands to a SQL (see below) database.

- **Data-definition query** – used to create, change, or delete tables in an Access database using SQL statements.

SQL stands for Structured Query Language, often used to query, update, and manage relational databases. Each query created by Access has an associated SQL statement that defines the action of that query. Thus, if you are familiar with SQL, you can use such statements to view and modify queries, or set form and report properties. However, these actions can be done more easily with the Access QBE (query-by-example) grid, to be discussed next. If you design union queries, pass-through queries, or data-definition queries, then you must use SQL statements, as these types of queries can not be designed with the QBE grid. Finally, to create a sub-query, you use the QBE grid, but you enter a SQL SELECT statement for criteria, as we shall see in the next QBE grid example.

The Query Window

The Query window is a graphical query-by-example (QBE) tool. Because of Access' graphical features, you can use the mouse to select, drag, and manipulate objects in the query window to define how you would like to see your data.

An example of a ready made Query window can be seen by opening the Find duplicates for Orders query (by double-clicking its entry in the Navigation Pane) and clicking the **Design View** button 📉 on the Status bar. This opens the Query window shown in Fig. 6.5.

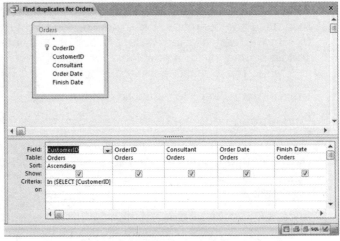

Fig. 6.5 A Select Query in Design View

You can add a table to the top half of the Query window by dragging the table from the Navigation Pane. Similarly, you can add fields to the bottom half of the Query window (the QBE grid) by dragging them from the tables on the top half of the Query window. Also, the QBE grid is used to select the data sort order, or insert criteria, such as SQL statements.

To see the full SQL statement written by Access as the criteria selection when we first defined the above query, click the **SQL View** button 🔤. This is shown in Fig. 6.6 on the next page.

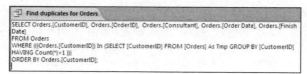

Fig. 6.6 The SQL Statement for our Query

Note the part of the statement which states 'As Tmp GROUP'. Access collects the data you want as a temporary group, called a *dynaset*. This special set of data behaves like a table, but is not a table; it is a dynamic view of the data from one or more tables, selected and sorted by the particular query.

Adding Tables to a Query Window

To explore more about query design, click the **Create**, **Other**, **Query Design** button, to open the Query window in Design View and the Show Table box shown below. The Invoices and Customers tables were then added to the Query window by selecting them in the Show Table box and pressing the **Add** button, as shown in Fig. 6.7.

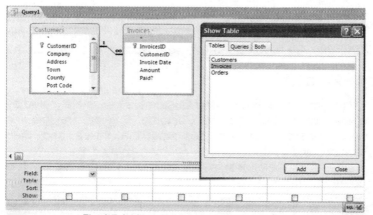

Fig. 6.7 Adding tables to the Query Window

Adding Fields to a Query Window

In Fig. 6.8 we show a screen in which the Paid?, InvoicesID, and Amount fields have been dragged from the Invoices table and added to the Query window. Also, the Company and Contact fields have been dragged from the Customers table and placed on the Query window, while the Phone field from the Customers table is about to be added to the Query window.

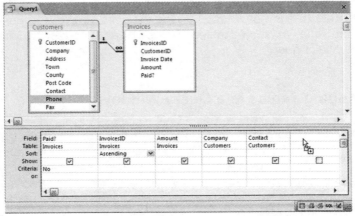

Fig. 6.8 Dragging Fields from Tables to the QBE Grid

Having dragged all six fields from the two tables onto the QBE grid, we have added the word **No** as the criteria on the Paid? field and selected **Ascending** as the Sort for the InvoicesID field.

Note that the Invoices and Customers tables are joined by a line that connects the two CustomerID fields. The join line was created when we designed the tables and their relationships in the previous chapter. Even if you have not created these relationships, Access will join the tables in a query automatically when the tables are added to a query, provided each table has a field with the same name and a compatible data type and one of those fields is a primary key. A primary key field is displayed with a 🔑 in the Query window.

Run

Clicking the **Query Tools**, **Design**, **Results**, **Run** button, shown here, instantly displays all the unpaid invoices with the details you have asked for, as follows:

Unpaid Invoices					
Paid?	InvoicesID	Amount	Company	Contact	Phone
☐	2	£1,232.00	PARKWAY Gravel	James Stone	01534 987654
☐	4	£876.00	GLOWORM Ltd	Peter Summers	01432 746523
☐	6	£326.00	WORMGLAZE Ltd	Richard Glazer	01123 654321
☐	8	£1,689.60	HIRE Service Equipment	Nicole Webb	01875 558822
☐	9	£1,053.00	EUROBASE Co. Ltd	Sarah Star	01736 098765
☐	11	£1,400.00	VORTEX Co. Ltd	Brian Storm	01776 223344
☐	12	£1,200.00	AVON Construction	John Waters	01657 113355
☐	13	£345.00	BARROWS Associates	Mandy Brown	01554 664422
☐	14	£657.50	SILVERSMITH Co	Adam Smith	01336 997755
☐	(New)				
Total	9	£8,779.10			

Fig. 6.9 Unpaid Invoices from the Adept Consultants Database

We also added a Totals row as described on page 148. To save your newly created query, right-click its tab and use the **Save** command, giving it a name such as 'Unpaid Invoices'.

Types of Criteria

Access accepts the following expressions as criteria:

Arithmetic Operators		Comparison Operators		Logical Operators	
*	Multiply	<	Less than	And	And
/	Divide	<=	Less than or equal	Or	Inclusive or
+	Add	>	Greater than	Xor	Exclusive or
-	Subtract	>=	Greater than or equal	Not	Not equivalent
		=	Equal	Eqv	Equivalent
		<>	Not equal	Imp	Implication
Other operators					
Between	Between 50 And 150	All values between 50 and 150			
In	In ("Bath","Bristol")	All records with Bath and Bristol			
Is	Is Null	All records with no value in that field			
Like	Like "Brian *"	All records with Brian something in field			
&	[Name]&" "&[Surname]	Concatenates strings			

Using Wildcard Characters in Criteria

In a previous example we used the criteria **W*** to mean any company whose name starts with the letter 'W'. The asterisk in this criteria is known as a wildcard character.

To search for a pattern, you can use the asterisk (*) and the question mark (?) as wildcard characters when specifying criteria in expressions. An asterisk stands for any number of characters, while a question mark stands for any single character in the same position as the question mark.

The following examples show the use of wildcard characters in various types of expressions. However, in a database field all words in that field are considered as an entity. Hence, if you were looking for all occurrences of Mary in, say, the Contact field, you should enter the criteria as Mary*. The asterisk indicates that there is more in that field.

Entered Expression	Meaning	Examples
a?	Any two-letter word beginning with A	am, an, as, at
???d	Any four-letter word ending with d	find, hand, land, yard
Sm?th	Any five-letter word beginning with Sm and ending with th	Smith, Smyth
fie*	Any word starting with the letters fie	field, fiend, fierce, fiery
*ght	Any word ending with ght	alight, eight, fight, light, might, sight
*/5/2007	All dates in May 2007	1/5/2007
a	Any word with the letter a in it	Brian, Mary, star, yard

Combining Criteria

By specifying additional criteria in a Query window you can create powerful queries for viewing your data.

The AND Criteria with Different Fields: When you insert criteria in several fields, but in the same row, Access assumes that you are searching for records that meet all of the criteria. For example, the criteria below lists the records shown in Fig. 6.10.

Field:	Paid?	InvoicesID	Amount	Company	Contact	Phone
Table:	Invoices	Invoices	Invoices	Customers	Customers	Customers
Sort:		Ascending				
Show:	☑	☑		☑	☑	☑
Criteria:	No		Between 300 and 900			
or:						

Unpaid Invoices

Paid?	InvoicesID	Amount	Company	Contact	Phone
☐	4	£876.00	GLOWORM Ltd	Peter Summers	01432 746523
☐	6	£326.00	WORMGLAZE Ltd	Richard Glazer	01123 654321
☐	13	£345.00	BARROWS Associates	Mandy Brown	01554 664422
☐	14	£657.50	SILVERSMITH Co	Adam Smith	01336 997755
* ☐	(New)				
Total	4	£2,204.50			

Fig. 6.10 Illustrating the AND Criteria with Different Fields

The OR Criteria with the Same Field: If you include multiple criteria in one field only, then Access assumes that you are searching for records that meet any one of the specified criteria. The criteria <300 or >1100 in the field Amount, shown in Fig. 6.11, list the required records, only if the No in the Paid? field is inserted in both rows.

Field:	Paid?	InvoicesID	Amount	Company	Contact	Phone
Table:	Invoices	Invoices	Invoices	Customers	Customers	Customers
Sort:		Ascending				
Show:	☑	☑	☑	☑	☑	☑
Criteria:	No		<300			
or:	No		>1100			

Unpaid Invoices

Paid?	InvoicesID	Amount	Company	Contact	Phone
☐	2	£1,232.00	PARKWAY Gravel	James Stone	01534 987654
☐	8	£1,689.60	HIRE Service Equipment	Nicole Webb	01875 558822
☐	11	£1,400.00	VORTEX Co. Ltd	Brian Storm	01776 223344
☐	12	£1,200.00	AVON Construction	John Waters	01657 113355
* ☐	(New)				
Total	4	£5,521.60			

Fig. 6.11 Illustrating the OR Criteria with the Same Field

The OR Criteria with Different Fields: If you include multiple criteria in different fields, but in different rows, then Access assumes that you are searching for records that meet either one or the other of the specified criteria. For example, the criteria Yes in the Paid? field and the criteria <600 in the Amount field, but in different rows, list the following records.

Field:	Paid?	InvoicesID	Amount	Company	Contact	Phone
Table:	Invoices	Invoices	Invoices	Customers	Customers	Customers
Sort:		Ascending				
Show:	☑	☑	☑	☑	☑	☑
Criteria:	Yes					
or:			<600			

Unpaid Invoices						
Paid?	InvoicesID	Amount	Company	Contact	Phone
☑	1	£450.87	STONEAGE Ltd	Mike Irons	01765 234567
☑	3	£543.90	WESTWOOD Ltd	Mary Slim	01234 667755
☑	5	£986.00	SILVERSMITH Co	Adam Smith	01336 997755
☐	6	£326.00	WORMGLAZE Ltd	Richard Glazer	01123 654321
☑	7	£478.98	EALING Engines Design	Trevor Miles	01336 010107
☑	10	£1,385.00	AVON Construction	John Waters	01657 113355
☐	13	£345.00	BARROWS Associates	Mandy Brown	01554 664422
☐	(New)				
Total	7	£4,515.75			

Fig. 6.12 Illustrating the OR Criteria with Different Fields

The AND and OR Criteria Together: The following choice of criteria gets Access to retrieve either records that have Yes in the Paid? field and the company's name starts with the letter A, or records that the invoice amount is less than £340.

Field:	Paid?	InvoicesID	Amount	Company	Contact	Phone
Table:	Invoices	Invoices	Invoices	Customers	Customers	Customers
Sort:		Ascending				
Show:	☑	☑	☑	☑	☑	☑
Criteria:	Yes			Like "A*"		
or:			<340			

Unpaid Invoices						
Paid?	InvoicesID	Amount	Company	Contact	Phone
☐	6	£326.00	WORMGLAZE Ltd	Richard Glazer	01123 654321
☑	10	£1,385.00	AVON Construction	John Waters	01657 113355
☐	(New)				
Total	2	£1,711.00			

Fig. 6.13 Illustrating the AND and OR Criteria together

Creating Calculated Fields

Let's assume that we want to increase the amounts payable on all invoices overdue by more than 60 days from today by 0.5%, as a penalty for not settling on time. We can achieve this by creating a calculated field in our database.

To create a calculated field, open the **Adept Consultants** database, double-click the Unpaid Invoices query entry `Unpaid Invoices` in the Navigation Pane to reopen the query, and click the **Design View** button on the Toolbar. Next, insert a field after the Amount field by highlighting the column to its right and clicking the **Design**, **Query Setup**, **Insert Columns** command button `Insert Columns`. Now type the following statement in the Field row of the newly inserted empty column, as shown in Fig. 6.14, below:

New Amount:[Amount]*1.005

where *New Amount:* is our chosen name for the calculated field – the colon is essential. If you do not supply a name for the calculated field, Access uses the default name *Expr1:*, which you can rename later. The square brackets enclosing the word Amount in the above expression indicate that it is an existing field name.

Field:	Paid?		InvoicesID	Invoice Date	[Invoice Date]+60	Amount	New Amount: [Amount]*1.005	Company	
Table:	Invoices		Invoices	Invoices		Invoices		Customers	
Sort:			Ascending						
Show:	☑		☑	☑	☐	☑	☑	☑	
Criteria:	No				<Date()				
or:									

Fig. 6.14 The Completed Query

Next, click the **Design**, **Show/Hide**, **Property Sheet** button, or right-click in the new field and select **Properties** from the context menu, and set the Format property of the new field to Currency as shown in Fig. 6.15 on the next page. Finally, create another column, type:

Due Date:[Invoice Date]+60

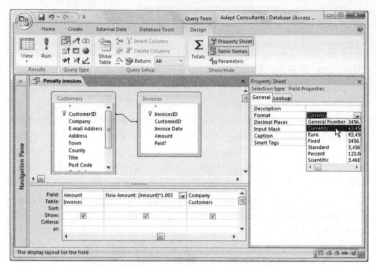

Fig. 6.15 Setting a Field's Properties to Currency

into its Field row and **<Date()** into its Criteria field, as we show in Fig. 6.14. We don't need this column to show in the result so have unchecked the **Show** check box.

Now, clicking either the **Datasheet View** button on the Status bar, or the **Design**, **Results**, **Run** button on the Ribbon, displays the following results:

Penalty invoices					
Paid? ▾	InvoicesID ▾	Invoice Date ▾	Amount ▾	New Amount ▾	Company ▾
☐	2	15/06/2007	£1,232.00	£1,238.16	PARKWAY Gravel
☐	4	28/07/2007	£876.00	£880.38	GLOWORM Ltd
☐	6	05/08/2007	£326.00	£327.63	WORMGLAZE Ltd
☐	8	12/08/2007	£1,689.60	£1,698.05	HIRE Service Equipment
☐	9	18/08/2007	£1,053.00	£1,058.27	EUROBASE Co Ltd
☐	11	01/09/2007	£1,400.00	£1,407.00	VORTEX Co. Ltd
☐	12	10/09/2007	£1,200.00	£1,206.00	AVON Construction
* ☐	(New)				
Total	7		£7,776.60		

Fig. 6.16 Results of the Penalty Invoices Query

We suggest you save this query under the name Penalty invoices. If the Total line does not show for you, just click the **Home**, **Records**, **Totals** button ∑ Totals, which toggles it on and off.

Simple Date Calculations

When you enter a date into an Access table, Access recognises it as a date, and checks it against the calendar to make sure it is a valid date. Then it stores the date as a number known as the date serial. PCs use the '1900 System' to store dates with 1st January 1900 as day 1, 2nd January day 2, etc. You don't need to know this date number but Access uses it in mathematical calculations.

In the expression in our last example:

Due Date:[Invoice Date]+60

Due Date: creates a new field called Due Date, and **[Invoice Date]+60** takes the date it finds in the Invoice Date field and adds 60 to its serial number.

The criteria expression we added to the Due Date field, **>Date()**, checks to see if the resulting date is earlier than the current date. 'Date()' is an Access function that returns the current date.

Using Functions in Criteria

Access has many other functions that you can use in a calculated field of an Access query which can be used for such things as, extracting information from text or date fields, or to calculate the totals of entries.

Finding Part of a Date Field

To extract part of the date field 'Date', such as the month in which unpaid invoices were issued, enter

Month:DatePart("m",[Date])

in the Field row of an empty field.

To extract the year in which unpaid invoices were issued, enter the following in the Field row of an empty field.

Year:DatePart("yyyy",[Date])

This function returns the year in four digits, such as 2007. The result of such a query is shown in Fig. 6.17 below.

Unpaid Invoices						
Paid?	InvoicesID	Invoice Date	Amount	Company	Month	Year
☐	2	15/06/2007	£1,232.00	PARKWAY Gravel	6	2007
☐	4	28/07/2007	£876.00	GLOWORM Ltd	7	2007
☑	6	05/08/2007	£326.00	WORMGLAZE Ltd	8	2007
☐	8	12/08/2007	£1,689.60	HIRE Service Equipment	8	2007
☐	9	18/08/2007	£1,053.00	EUROBASE Co Ltd	8	2007
☐	11	01/09/2007	£1,400.00	VORTEX Co. Ltd	9	2007
☐	12	10/09/2007	£1,200.00	AVON Construction	9	2007
☐	13	26/09/2007	£345.00	BARROWS Associates	9	2007
☐	14	10/10/2007	£657.50	SILVERSMITH Co	10	2007
* ☐	(New)					
Total	9		£8,779.10			

Fig. 6.17 Results of the DatePart Queries

Finding Part of a Text Field

Let us assume that you want to find information that is part of a text field, like the area code (first 5 numbers) in the Phone field of our Customers table. To help you search a table for only part of a text field, Access provides three string functions. The syntax of these functions is as follows:

Left(stringexpr,n)
Right(stringexpr,n)
Mid(stringexpr,start,n)

The *stringexpr* argument can be either a field name or a text expression, while *n* is the number of characters you are searching for, and *start* is the position of the first character you want to start from.

Thus, to extract the area code of the text field Phone in our Customers table, open the Unpaid Invoices query, click the **Design View** button on the Status bar, and type in the Field row of an empty field, either

Area Codes:Left([Phone],5)
or
Area Codes:Mid([Phone],1,5)

Note that to distinguish between the name of a field and a text expression, the name of the field is enclosed in square brackets.

Next, click the **Datasheet View** button on the Status bar. The result of such a query is displayed in Fig. 6.18 below.

Fig. 6.18 Results of the Area Codes Query

Calculating Totals in Queries

Sometimes you might want the total value of outstanding invoices grouped by months. Access allows you to perform calculations on groups of records using *totals* queries, also known as *aggregate* queries.

Function	Used to Find
Avg	The average of values in a field
Count	The number of values in a field
First	The field value from the first record in a table or query
Last	The field value from the last record in a table or query
Max	The highest value in a field
Min	The lowest value in a field
StDev	The standard deviation of values in a field
Sum	The total of values in a field
Var	The variance of values in a field

The table on the previous page lists the functions that can be used in queries to display totals. These functions are entered in the Totals row of a query which can be displayed by clicking the **Design**, **Show/Hide**, **Totals** button, shown in Fig. 6.19 below, while in Design View.

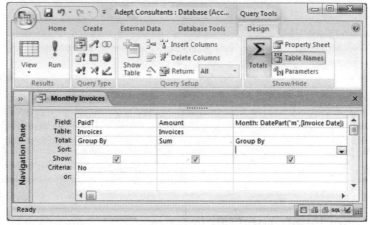

Fig. 6.19 Using the Sum Total Function in a Query

The retrieved records from this query which we have named 'Monthly Invoices' are shown in Fig. 6.20 below.

Paid?	SumOfAmount	Month
☐	£1,232.00	6
☐	£876.00	7
☐	£3,068.60	8
☐	£2,945.00	9
☐	£657.50	10

Fig. 6.20 Results of the Monthly Invoices Query

The Expression Builder

So far we have seen that operators, criteria and functions can be used to create an expression in an Access query and we have manually typed them into the QBE grid. There is another way to write expressions or call built-in functions which is a little easier and helps to reduce mistakes. Access 2007 is equipped with an Expression Builder.

Fig. 6.21 The Expression Builder

To access the Expression Builder from a query window in Design View, select the field cell where you want the expression and either click the **Design**, **Query Setup**, **Builder** button, or right-click and select **Build** from the context menu.

For other Access controls, open the Properties window for the control that will use the expression or function you want to build, and click its ellipsis button.

The text box under the Title bar is the expression area, used to show the current expression. You can type directly into this or use the options below to add to the expression being built.

Below the expression area is a row of operator buttons. To use one of these operators in your expression, you click its button. Sometimes when you click a button, Access adds the placeholder «Expr». You must then replace this with a valid value, expression, or function.

Under the button bar, there are three list boxes. The left list displays categories of items, such as the objects in the current database and available functions. To access a database object expand it by clicking the folder button 🗀 next to it, or by double-clicking its ⊞ button. Selecting an object in the left list, opens a list of available options in the middle list. To use a control from the middle list in your expression you can double-click it. The name of the control then appears in the expression area. Clicking an object in the middle pane opens a sub-list in the right pane.

For instance, to access one of the Access built-in functions, expand the **Functions** node in the left list and click **Built-In Functions**. The middle list then displays the available function categories. Clicking one of these shows the available functions in the right list. You then either click the one you want to select it and click the **Paste** button, or just double-click it, to place the function in the expression area, as shown in Fig. 6.21.

If the added function expects arguments, its name and a placeholder for each argument will be added to the expression area. You then have to replace each placeholder with a suitable value or expression. To help here, the Expression Builder shows the syntax of the function on its Status bar. To get more help, click the **Help** button which opens a detailed page on the function or operation being attempted, as shown in Fig. 6.22 on the next page.

After creating your expression, if you are satisfied with it, click the **OK** button to place it in the query.

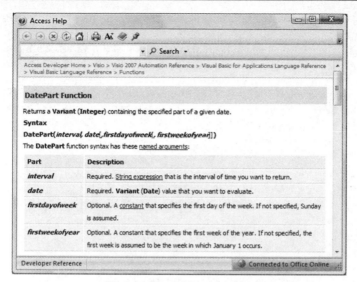

Fig. 6.22 Detailed Function Help

Up to now we have seen how to create a query with fields taken from two tables. To make it easier to see which field in a query comes from which table, Access displays the name of the table by default. This option is controlled with the **Design**, **Show/Hide**, **Table Names** button when in Design View. When this button is clicked, Access adds the Table row in the QBE grid, as shown in Fig. 6.23 below.

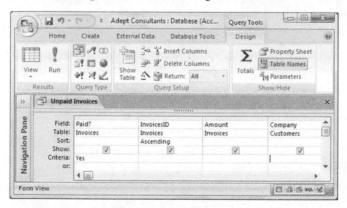

Fig. 6.23 The Table Names Control Button

Show Table

Now, suppose we would like to add the Orders table so that we can see the OrderID field in the extracted records of our query. To do this, click the **Design**, **Query Setup**, **Show Table** button, shown here, which opens the Show Table dialogue box we saw earlier in Fig. 6.7. In this box, select Orders and click the **Add** button, then drag the OrderID field onto the QBE grid, as shown in Fig. 7.2 below.

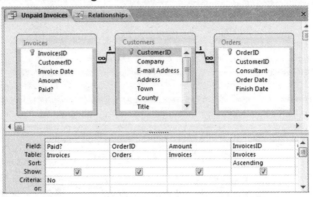

Fig. 6.24 The OrderID Field Added to the Query Grid

To find out what type of join exists between two tables, click the join line to highlight it, and select **Join Properties** from the shortcut menu. This will open the following dialogue box, in which we need option 2. Select it so that the Query will extract the correct records.

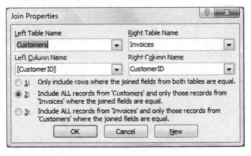

Fig. 6.25 The Join Properties Dialogue Box

Types of Joins

Microsoft Access supports the following types of joins:

Join Types	Effect
Equi-joins or Inner joins	A join in which records from two tables are combined and added to a dynaset only when there are equal values in the joined fields. For example, you can find records that show orders placed by each customer, with the dynaset containing only records for customers who have placed orders.
Outer joins	A join in which all the records from one table are added to the dynaset, and only those records from the other table for which values in the joined fields are equal. For example, you can find records that show all customers together with any orders they have placed.
Self-joins	A join in which records from one table are combined with other records from the same table when there are matching values in the joined fields. A self-join can be an equi-join or an outer join.

For an inner join, select option 1 from the Join Properties dialogue box. For an outer join, select option 2 or 3, depending on which records you want to include.

For example, choosing option 2 (also called a *left outer join*), displays all the required records from the Customers table and only those records from Orders where the joined fields are equal. Option 3 (also called a *right outer join*), on the other hand, attempts to display all records in Orders and only those records from Customers where the joined fields are equal, resulting in some confusion in our particular example.

Creating a Parameter Query

A *Parameter Query* is a variation of the *Select Query* – the type we have been using so far. A Parameter Query is used when you frequently run the same query, but need to change the criteria each time you run it. Instead of having to make changes to the QBE grid, Access prompts you for criteria. This type of query is particularly useful when used as a filter with forms.

To design a Parameter Query, design a new query in the normal way (without the Query Wizard), or change an existing Select Query. We have chosen the latter route and selected to change the Penalty invoices query. In Design View, this now looks as follows:

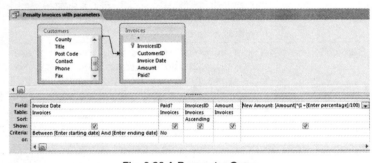

Fig. 6.26 A Parameter Query

Note the two changes made to the original query. In the Invoice Date field we have entered two prompts (in square brackets) in the Criteria row, namely

[Enter starting date]
[Enter ending date]

and in the calculated field we have replaced the *1.005 by

*(1+[Percentage]/100)

When working with expressions like these, that are longer than the visible cell space available, it is often easier to use the Zoom window opened into the cell with the **Shift+F2** key strokes.

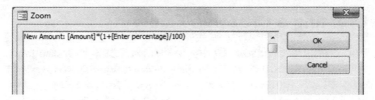

Fig. 6.27 Using a Zoom Window

When this query is run, Access asks for input values in three successive Enter Parameter Value boxes, as shown in Fig. 6.28 below.

Fig. 6.28 Entering the Three Parameters into the Query

Providing the appropriate input information, displays the result of this query, as follows:

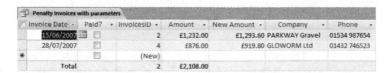

Fig. 6.29 The Query Results

We have saved the query under the name 'Penalty invoices with parameters'.

Creating a Crosstab Query

You create a *Crosstab Query* to display totals in a compact, spreadsheet format. A Crosstab query can present a large amount of summary data in a more readable form. The layout of the extracted data from such a query is ideal as the basis for a report.

For example, suppose we wanted to examine which of our employees was responsible for our customers' orders in each month. The information is contained in the Orders table of our database as shown in Fig. 6.30 below.

OrderID	CustomerID	Consultant	Order Date	Finish Date
1	STONEAGE Ltd	CH Wills	10/06/2007	13/07/2006
2	PARKWAY Gravel	AD Smith	15/06/2007	02/08/2007
3	WESTWOOD Ltd	WA Brown	16/07/2007	03/08/2007
4	GLOWORM Ltd	LS Stevens	28/07/2007	26/08/2007
5	SILVERSMITH Co	SF Adams	02/08/2007	18/08/2007
6	WORMGLAZE Ltd	CH Wills	05/08/2007	21/08/2007
7	EALING Engines Design	AD Smith	10/08/2007	17/10/2007
8	HIRE Service Equipment	WA Brown	12/08/2007	21/08/2007
9	EUROBASE Co Ltd	LS Stevens	18/08/2007	17/09/2007
10	AVON Construction	SF Adams	23/08/2007	24/09/2007
11	VORTEX Co. Ltd	AD Smith	01/09/2007	02/10/2007
12	AVON Construction	WA Brown	10/09/2007	09/10/2007
13	BARROWS Associates	SF Adams	26/09/2007	18/10/2007
14	SILVERSMITH Co	CH Wills	10/10/2007	22/10/2007

Record: 1 of 14 — No Filter — Search

Fig. 6.30 The Orders Table Sorted on Order Date

From the way this information is presented it is very difficult to work out who was responsible for which order in a given month. However, a Crosstab query that lists the names of the employees in rows and each month as a column heading, might be a better way to present this type of information.

To create a Crosstab query, open the **Adept Consultants** database, click the **Create**, **Other**, **Query Wizard** button and select the **Crosstab Query Wizard** option as shown in Fig. 6.31 on the next page.

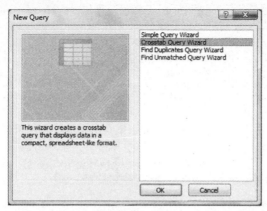

Fig. 6.31 Starting the Crosstab Query Wizard

Pressing the **OK** button, opens the Crosstab Query Wizard dialogue box. From this, select Orders from the displayed list of **Tables** and press the **Next** button.

From the next dialogue box, shown in Fig. 6.32 below, select a maximum of three fields from the displayed list, which will become the row headings of the crosstab form. Choose OrderID, CustomerID, and Consultant, in that order. The order you select these fields is important as Access will list the results of the query in alphabetical order of the first selected field.

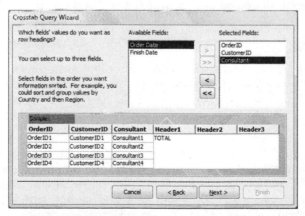

Fig. 6.32 Selecting Fields for the Crosstab Query

Having selected the three fields, click the **Next** button, and choose Order Date as the field whose value you want as the column headings. Press **Next**, select Month as the time interval by which you want to group your columns and press **Next** again. On the following dialogue box choose Count from the **Functions** list and press **Next**. Finally, accept the default name for the query, and press **Finish**.

The results of this Crosstab query are shown in Fig. 6.33 below with column widths set to Best Fit and empty columns hidden.

Orders_Crosstab									
OrderID ▾	CustomerID ▾	Consultant ▾	Total ▾	Jun ▾	Jul ▾	Aug ▾	Sep ▾	Oct ▾
1	STONEAGE Ltd	CH Wills	1	1				
2	PARKWAY Gravel	AD Smith	1	1				
3	WESTWOOD Ltd	WA Brown	1		1			
4	GLOWORM Ltd	LS Stevens	1		1			
5	SILVERSMITH Co	SF Adams	1			1		
6	WORMGLAZE Ltd	CH Wills	1			1		
7	EALING Engines Design	AD Smith	1			1		
8	HIRE Service Equipment	WA Brown	1			1		
9	EUROBASE Co Ltd	LS Stevens	1			1		
10	AVON Construction	SF Adams	1			1		
11	VORTEX Co. Ltd	AD Smith	1				1	
12	AVON Construction	WA Brown	1				1	
13	BARROWS Associates	SF Adams	1				1	
14	SILVERSMITH Co	CH Wills	1					1

Fig. 6.33 The Crosstab Query Results

As you can see from the above screen, the required information is tabulated and is extremely easy to read. However, the displayed recordset is not updatable.

To see the underlying structure of the query, click the **Design View** button to display the QBE grid, as follows:

Field:	[OrderID]	[CustomerID]	[Consultant]	Format([Order Date],"mmm")	[Finish Date]	Total Of Finish Date: [Finish Date]
Table:	Orders	Orders	Orders		Orders	Orders
Total:	Group By	Group By	Group By	Group By	Count	Count
Crosstab:	Row Heading	Row Heading	Row Heading	Column Heading	Value ▾	Row Heading
Sort:					Row Heading	
Criteria:					Column Heading	
or:					Value	
					(not shown)	

Fig. 6.34 The Crosstab Query in Design View

If you want to use a field for grouping, sorting, or setting criteria, but to exclude the field from the recordset, click the arrow in that field's Crosstab cell, and select **(not shown)** from the displayed list, as shown in Fig. 6.34 above.

Creating Queries for Updating Records

When a query is based on either a single table or on two tables with a one-to-one relationship, all the fields in the query can be edited and are updatable.

Queries which include more than one table, when some of the tables have a one-to-many relationship, are more difficult to design so that they are updatable.

The easiest way of finding out whether you can update records from a query, is to design the query, run it and try to change values in its various fields and also add data. If the table is updatable Access will let you make these changes, if not you will simply not be allowed to edit it.

All other types of queries, such as a Crosstab query, a query with totals, a query with Unique Values property set to Yes, a Union query, a Pass-through query, a calculated or read-only field, can not be used to update data.

To find out more, we suggest you look up the 'Edit data in a query?' section in Access Help, as shown in Fig. 6.35.

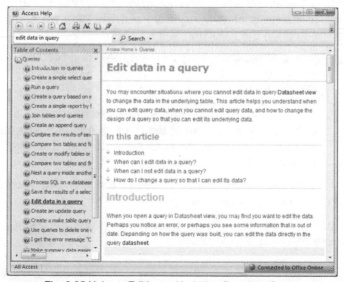

Fig. 6.35 Help on Editing or Updating Data in a Query

Creating Action Queries

You can create *Action Queries* in the same way as Select Queries. Action Queries are used to make bulk changes to data rather than simply displaying data. For this reason, Action Queries can be dangerous for the novice, simply because they change your database.

There are four different types of Action Queries, with the following functions:

Type of Query	Function
Append query	Adds records from one or more tables to another table or tables.
Delete query	Deletes records from a table or tables.
Make-table query	Creates a new table from all or part of another table or tables.
Update query	Changes the data in a group of records

In an earlier version of Access, you could quickly create an Action query which moved old orders to an Old Orders Archive table, by using the Archive Query Wizard. If you want to design such a query from scratch, then we suggest you go through the following steps:

- Use a Make-table query to copy selected records from an existing table into a new table, named, say, Old Orders Archive.

- Change the design of the Make-table query so that on subsequent execution of the query it Appends selected records from your original table to the Old Orders Archive table.

- Use the Delete query to delete the archived records from the original table.

In what follows, we will go through the steps necessary to create an Old Orders Archive query.

If necessary, open the **Adept Consultants** database and click the **Design**, **Other**, **Query Design** button to create a new query in Design View.

In the Show Table box that opens next (Fig. 6.36), select Orders, as shown here, then press the **Add** button, followed by the **Close** button.

Fig. 6.36 The Show Table Box

This adds the Orders table to the Select Query window which also contains the QBE grid, so that you can design an appropriate query.

Drag all the fields from the Orders table onto the QBE grid, and add in the Order Date field the criteria <=5/8/07, as shown in Fig. 6.37 below.

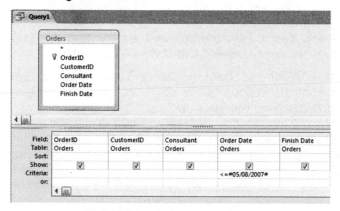

Fig. 6.37 Creating a Make Table Query

Click the **Design**, **Query Type**, **Make Table** button on the Ribbon, shown highlighted here, which opens the Make Table dialogue box shown in Fig. 6.38 overleaf.

Finally, type the name of the new table, say, Old Orders Archive, and press **OK**.

Fig. 6.38 The Make Table Dialogue Box

If you press the **Design**, **Results**, **Run** button a warning box is displayed. In our example, we are told that six records are about to be pasted onto our new table, as shown in Fig. 6.39.

Fig. 6.39 An Access Warning Message

Pressing **Yes**, copies the selected records from the Orders table to the newly created Old Orders Archive table.

Next, action the **Design**, **Query Type**, **Append** button. The Append dialogue box is displayed with the Old Orders Archive name appearing as default. Press **OK** and close the Append Query window. When you click the ▬✕▬ button to close the Append Query window, you will be asked whether you would like your design to be saved. Select **Yes**, and in the displayed Save As dialogue box, type the new name for the query. We chose to call it Append to Old Orders Archive.

As an exercise, you could go through the steps of designing another Make Table query, but select the **Delete** option of the Query Type menu. This would be used to delete old records from the Orders table once they have been moved to the Old Orders Archive table, but see the next page first.

The next time you look in the Navigation Pane you should see that Access has placed a new table in the Table list, and a new query in the Query list, as shown in Fig. 6.40 below. The query has an exclamation mark attached to its icon so that you don't run it inadvertently.

All Access Objects ▾ «
Tables ⌃
   Customers
   Invoices
   Old Orders Archive
   Orders
Queries ⌃
   Append to Old Orders Archive
   Orders_Crosstab
   Find duplicates for Orders
   Monthly Invoices
   Penalty invoices
   Penalty invoices with parameters
   Totals in query
   Unpaid Invoices
Forms ⌄

Fig. 6.40 The New Action Query and Table in the Navigation Pane

In all, there are four Action queries available in Access, with the following functions.

1   The **Make-Table** query; used to create a table by retrieving the records that meet certain criteria and using them to create a new table.

2   The **Append** query; used to append (add) records from one table to another existing table.

3   The **Update** query; used to change data in existing tables, such as the cost per hour charged to your customers.

4   The **Delete** query; used to delete (remove) records that meet certain pre-defined criteria from a table.

Getting More Help

As we are sure you have found by now, the Help section of Access is essential reading when you are tackling a new feature. We strongly recommend that you work your way through the sections on Queries and Functions.

Below is a typical example of the depth of detail in some of the Help screens.

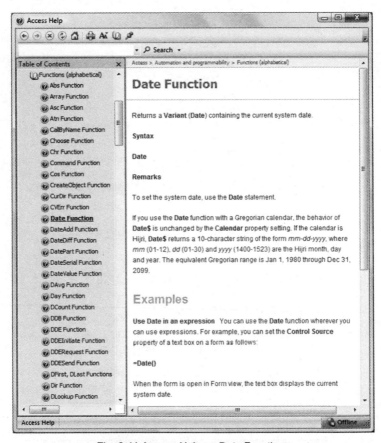

Fig. 6.41 Access Help on Date Functions

7

Rich Text Formatting

Rich text formatting, or RTF, is a proprietary document file format developed by Microsoft in 1987 for cross-platform document interchange. It is a way of encoding various text formatting properties, such as bold and italic characters, different typefaces and colours.

In Access 2007, you can now set a 'Memo' field in a table to support rich text formatting and then apply rich text formatting to the data in that field. So you can now format the data in your tables and query result sets, as well as in text boxes on forms and reports as long as they are 'bound' to the Memo fields in your tables. The types of formatting available are shown in the Help table in Fig. 7.1 on the next page. Not all the usual Office 2007 formatting is available, but this is a great improvement on previous versions of Access.

The procedure, however, for setting up your tables and fields to make use of rich text formatting is, to say the least, 'anything but intuitive'. If you don't follow it you are likely to get extremely frustrated!

Just in case you are interested, Access 2007 does not actually save your data in **.rtf** format, but uses Hypertext Markup Language (HTML) formatting code. This apparently gives more compatibility with the rich text fields in Microsoft's SharePoint Services 3.0 lists.

Enabling Rich Text Formatting

You can enable rich text editing only for fields set to the Memo data type in Access 2007 tables. After you add a memo field to a table, you enable rich text formatting by setting its **Text Format** property, as we shall see.

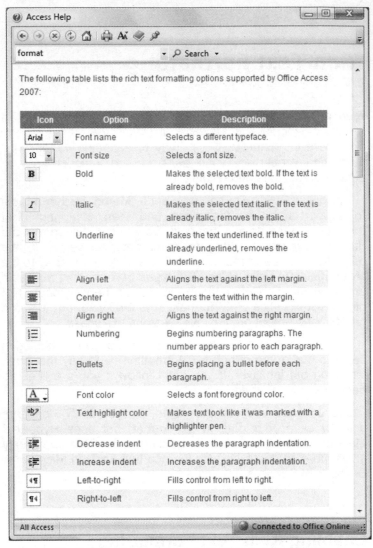

Fig. 7.1 The Rich Text Formats Available in Access 2007

The RTF formatting commands above can be found in the **Font** and **Rich Text** groups on the **Home** tab, and in the Mini toolbar (when it opens).

Adding a Memo Field

To add a new field to an existing table, open the table in Datasheet View by double-clicking its entry in the Navigation Pane, select a blank field, double-click the field header and enter a name for the new field.

To set its data type in Datasheet View, select **Memo** from the **Datasheet**, **Data Type & Formatting**, **Data Type** drop down list.

Setting the Text Format

In our example below we have created a new table in a new database, with both being called Quotations. We shall store the quotations of some well-known people there. We show the simple structure of the table in Design View.

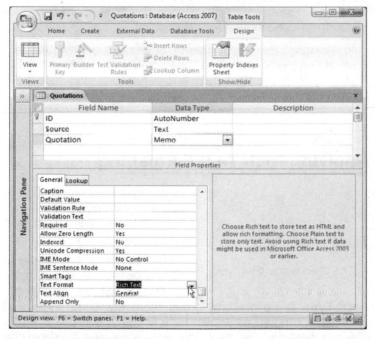

Fig. 7.2 Setting the Text Format Property of a Memo Field

You can see that we have set the Quotation Data Type cell as Memo and with the cell still selected have clicked the General tab in the Field Properties section. Next we clicked the list to the right of the **Text Format** property box, and selected **Rich Text**.

For us this opened a Warning dialogue box telling us the field will be converted to Rich Text. As this is exactly what we want we clicked the **Yes** button and used the **Office Button** , **Save** command to save the table details. That's all there is to it. A pity there are no commands on the Ribbon for this!

The Append Only Property

If you attempt to enable rich text editing for an existing table, you might find that the table has the **Append Only** property enabled. This has to be disabled or Access hides the text in the field whenever you place your cursor in that field, or in any form controls bound to that field.

In Design View this property is located below the **Text Format** property we have just looked at and shown in Fig. 7.2. Click the field next to the property and select **No** from the list.

Applying Rich Text Formatting

Fig. 7.3 Checking the Data Type

To add text to a memo field in Datasheet View, click the cell in the field you want, and then just type in the text.

To check that it is a memo field (in Datasheet View), open the **Datasheet** tab and in the **Data Type & Formatting** group, note the **Data Type** that appears in the list, as shown here in Fig. 7.3. As you select different fields in the table this entry changes to show the data types of the fields.

Fig. 7.4 Applying Rich Text Formats in Memo Field

Once you have entered the text data in a field you can then format it in much the same way as you would in your favourite word processor, as the formatting tools in Access work like the tools in other programs. Access uses the standard Office 2007 buttons for formatting and aligning text, and for formatting rich text. You can select a different font, make the text bold, italic or underlined, apply a colour to it, or change your text alignment, and so on.

Formatting commands are located in the **Font** and **Rich Text** groups of the **Home** tab, and in the Mini toolbar that appears whenever you highlight part or all of the text in a field. These commands are all described in Fig. 7.1 and shown being used in our example in Fig. 7.4 above.

Formatting changes to the database are automatically saved when you move the pointer to another table field. You can also use the **Shift+Enter** keyboard shortcut which also moves the entry point to the end of the current entry.

Different Access Views

So far we have considered rich text formatting in database tables (or query result sets) in Datasheet View, but once you have created a memo field and set its **Text Format** to **Rich Text** you can see the formatting in forms and reports. In fact these are really the areas where the feature is of most use.

You can also add the RTF formatting in some database views, as follows:

Forms open in Form View – You can apply formatting to part or all of the text in a memo field.

Forms open in Layout View – You can use a smaller number of the commands, and your changes apply to all of the text in the text box that displays the data. You cannot format individual letters or blocks of text while working in Layout View.

Reports open in Layout View – Like forms open in Layout View, Access 2007 provides a smaller number of commands, and any changes you make apply to the entire memo field.

8

Using Forms

In this chapter, we introduce the subject of Forms and show you how to create and use them in Access 2007.

The Access Datasheets and Queries we have spent time on so far, show 'spreadsheet like' views of the data in a database with each record taking up a row and each field a column. Forms, on the other hand, can show the data one record at a time, and you can control what fields are contained on a form and how they are displayed.

Forms let you find, edit, and add data to your database in a convenient manner. Forms look good on screen, but do not produce very good output on paper. Access provides you with an easy way of designing various types of forms, some of which are discussed here.

Creating Forms

We saw in an earlier chapter (page 63) how easy it was to create a form to view our Customers table. To see this again, go back to page 63, or 'in real life', open **Adept Consultants** in Access 2007 and in the Navigation Pane double-click the **Customers** form button  in the Customers section. If you didn't save it, don't worry you can easily create it again by opening the Customers table and clicking the **Create**, **Forms**, **Form** button.

Fig. 8.1 The Forms Group

The controls for creating forms are located in the **Create**, **Forms** group, as shown here.

As you can see, there are several different types of forms available for you to choose from.

Using the Form Wizard

You can use the Form Wizard to easily create a form from data in either a table or a query. Clicking the **Create**, **Forms**, **More Forms**, **Form Wizard** command opens the Wizard.

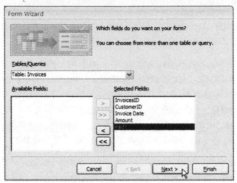

Fig. 8.2 Creating a Form with the Form Wizard

The first Wizard window, shown in Fig. 8.2 asks you to specify what fields contain the data to be included in the form. We chose all the fields in the Invoices table, by clicking the ⮞⮞ button followed by the **Next** button to move to the next Wizard window.

In the next three windows displayed by the Wizard, we made the following selections in order of appearance:

- **Columnar** for the layout of the form.

- **Module** as the style for Labels and Data.

- **Open the form to View or enter information**.

Pressing the **Finish** button displayed the completed form shown in Fig. 8.3 on the next page (after about one and a half minutes).

Using the Form Wizard lets you be more selective about what fields appear in a form. You can also define how the data is grouped and sorted, and can use fields from more than one table or query, provided the relationships between them have already been established.

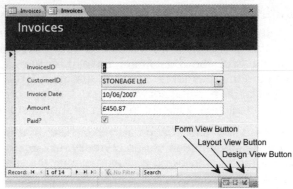

Fig. 8.3 The Invoices Form in Form View

Types of Forms

Access 2007 can create many different types of forms for you to work with, using the following commands:

Form Control	Function
Form Design	Designs a form from scratch.
Form	Creates a simple form very quickly.
Split Form	Creates a form with a datasheet and form together Viewing the same data.
Multiple Items	Creates a form with multiple records in a Datasheet View.
More Forms	Including the Form Wizard which automatically creates a form based on your selected choices.

Access also allows you to design a form that contains another form. This type of form, called main/subform, allows data from related tables to be viewed at the same time.

Subforms are especially effective when you want to show data from tables or queries with a one-to-many relationship. For example, as we show next, you can create a form with a subform to show data from a Customers table and an Invoices table, where each customer can be issued with more than one invoice.

Creating a Form with a Subform

To help us enter new invoice data into our **Adept Consultants** database we will build a new form which holds the fields from the Customers table, but has a subform holding the Invoices table. So when the main form shows all the details of a particular customer, the subform will be visible with all the invoice information for that customer.

Before doing this you must make sure that your table relationships have been set up correctly. In our example, as long as you have followed our instructions, there should not be too many problems!

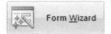 As before, click the **Create**, **Forms**, **More Forms**, **Form Wizard** button to open the Wizard, and in the first wizard dialogue box, shown in Fig. 8.4 below, select the Customers table as shown. The two tables we are going to use have a one-to-many relationship, and Customers is the 'one' side of this one-to-many relationship. In other words, every customer can have many invoices, but each invoice will only be relevant to one customer.

Double-click all the fields in the **Available Fields** list to move them to the **Selected Fields** box, as shown.

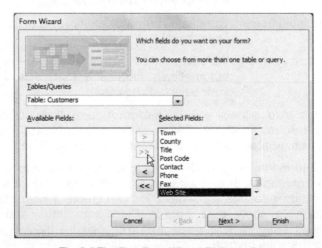

Fig. 8.4 The First Form Wizard Dialogue Box

Next, in the **same** wizard dialogue box, select the Invoices table from the **Tables/Queries** list and select all the fields except CustomerID, then click the **Next** button.

As long as you have set up the relationships correctly before starting the procedure, the next wizard box (Fig. 8.5), asks which table or query you want to view by. In our case, to create the Customers form, click **by Customers**. In the same dialogue box, select the **Form with subform(s)** option, as shown below and click the **Next** button.

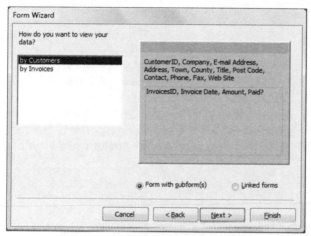

Fig. 8.5 The Second Form Wizard Dialogue Box

Select **Datasheet** layout and choose a style you like in the next two wizard dialogue boxes (not shown here), and name the **Form** Customer Invoice Details in the last box, shown in Fig. 8.6 on the next page. We chose the Access 2007 style for our form, but you can obviously experiment here. Be warned though, for us the style examples shown on the dialogue box did not always bear much resemblance to the finished form. Strange!

When you click **Finish**, Access creates two forms, one for the main form and subform control, and one for the subform, and opens the new form shown in Fig. 8.7, also on the next page.

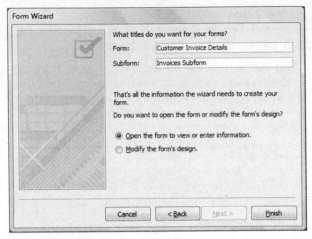

Fig. 8.6 The Last Form Wizard Dialogue Box

It's as easy as that with Access 2007. The form produced almost automatically is by no means perfect, but for most people would be adequate. We will customise it later on.

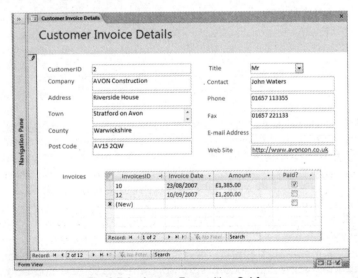

Fig. 8.7 An Access Form with a Subform

Access Form Views

Form View

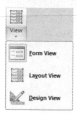

When you first open a form in a database it is opened in Form View. In this view you search, view, add to and edit your data.

Access 2007 has two other 'views' you can use for customising forms and reports once they are created. These are all accessed from the **Views** buttons on the Status bar, shown in Fig. 8.3, or by clicking the down arrow under the **Home**, **Views**, **View** button and selecting from the drop-down list shown here.

Clicking the **View** button itself will always return you to the previous view used. You can see what that is by looking at the icon image on the button. In our example above, clicking the button would return you to Layout View.

Layout View

This is the most intuitive view to use, as you can see the data as it will appear in Form View, but also make changes to the form design. This is very useful for moving and re-sizing controls, as you can actually drag them around the form complete with the data being shown. This view may well be all you will need.

Design View

Some design operations are not possible in Layout View and require you to switch to Design View, which gives you a more detailed view of the structure of your form. You can see and change the Header, Detail, and Footer sections of the form, as well as add labels, images, lines, rectangles and other Visual Basic type controls. This view opens the **Design** and **Arrange** contextual tabs on the Ribbon and gives you access to the form Controls we shall see later.

Customising a Form

You can customise a form by changing the appearance of text, data, and any other attributes. In Fig. 8.8 below we show part of a slightly modified version of the Customer Invoice Details form in Layout View. It is in this view that you make any changes to the layout of the form.

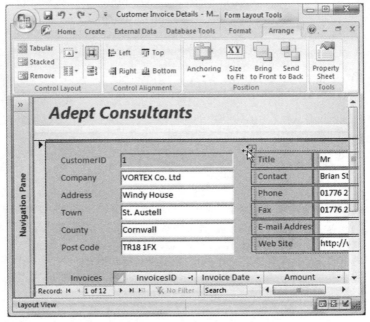

Fig. 8.8 Customising a Form in Layout View

Control Layout

When our form was created by the Form Wizard, the cells on it were automatically given a Stacked Layout. For example, clicking in a cell, such as the Contact box above, places orange lines around all the cells in the stack, as shown in Fig. 8.8. Any layout changes you then make affect the whole of the selected stack. In our example above all the cells to the right are being dragged around the form. Control layouts can be either tabular or stacked.

With tabular layouts (page 151), controls are arranged in rows and columns like a spreadsheet, with labels across the top. With stacked layouts, as in our example, controls are arranged vertically, with a label to the left of each control.

 You can set the layout of your form controls with the buttons on the **Arrange**, **Control Layout** group shown here.

Removing a control from a control layout allows you to set its size independently, or to place it anywhere on the form without affecting the positioning of any of the other stacked controls. To do this, select the control you want to remove and click the **Arrange**, **Control Layout**, **Remove** button. To select multiple controls, hold down the **Shift** key as you click the controls you want to select.

You can move a control within a control layout by dragging it to the location you want. As you drag the field, a horizontal or vertical bar indicates where it will be placed when you release the mouse button.

You can also move a control from one control layout to another control layout of the same type on the same form. In Fig. 8.9 for example, we are dragging the Title control from the bottom of the left stacked layout to the top of the right stacked layout, for very obvious reasons.

CustomerID	1		
Company	VORTEX Co. Ltd	Contact	Brian Storm
Address	Windy House	Phone	01776 223344
Town	St. Austell	Fax	01776 224466
County	Cornwall	E-mail Address	
Post Code	TR18 1FX	Web Site	http://www.vortex.com
Title	Mr		

Fig. 8.9 Moving a Control from One Layout to Another

When you move the pointer over a selected control it changes to a ✛ shape. This means you can then depress the left mouse button and drag the selection to move it.

To change the shape or re-size a selection you move the pointer over the side or corner you want to drag. It changes to a two-headed arrow (↔ ↕ ⬉) which you drag left or right, or up or down, to get the size of control you want, as shown in Fig. 8.10 below.

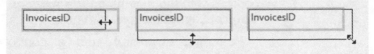

Fig. 8.10 Re-sizing a Form Control

Do try and experiment with moving and sizing label and data box controls and also changing their font and size (with the **Format**, **Font** options). If you don't like the result, simply don't save it. Skills gained here will be used in the Report design section later on.

Form Design

Access 2007 actually makes it fairly easy for you to design forms from scratch without using the Form Wizard. You start this process by clicking the **Create**, **Forms**, **Form Design** button which creates a new blank form and switches you to Design View, as shown in Fig. 8.11 on the facing page.

The Field List Pane

Here we have also opened the Field List pane by clicking the **Design**, **Tools**, **Add Existing Fields** toggle button shown here. We could also have used the **Alt+F8** keyboard shortcut. This is where you locate the fields you want to add to your form.

In the Field List pane, find the table containing the field you want to add to the form and access its list of fields by clicking the plus (+) or minus (−) signs next to it.

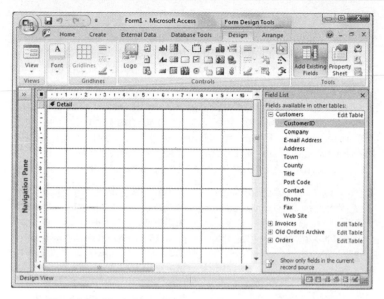

Fig. 8.11 A Blank Access Form with the Field List Pane Open

To add fields to your form either double-click them in the Field List pane, or drag them from the list to the form area.

Now the clever bit. Access creates appropriate controls on the form to display each field, binds the controls to their fields and creates labels for each control.

You will obviously have to arrange the controls and labels on the form area and possibly edit the labels by clicking to select them, and then clicking again to place the insertion point in them. Then, you can just type a new label straight in.

Access does its best to work out the type of controls that best fit your data, but if you want a field displayed in a different type of control you can easily change it. In Design View, right-click the control you want to change, and select **Change To** from the context menu. Click one of the available control types to change the control to that type. The control remains bound to the field, but you might have to set some properties to make the new control type work the way you want.

Object Properties

Forms and all the objects on the form have a list of properties associated with them, and you set these properties using a property sheet. These properties vary depending on the object.

To open the Property Sheet for an object in Design View, first click it to select the object and then either click the **Design**, **Tools**, **Property Sheet** toggle button, or press **F4**, or double-click the ■ button in the top-left section under the tab, or right-click and select the **Properties** option.

Property Sheet	×
Selection type: Form	
Form	▾

Format	Data	Event	Other	All

Record Source	▾ ...
Caption	
Pop Up	No
Modal	No
Display on SharePoint	Follow Table Setting
Default View	Single Form
Allow Form View	Yes
Allow Datasheet View	Yes
Allow PivotTable View	Yes
Allow PivotChart View	Yes
Allow Layout View	Yes
Picture	(none)
Picture Tiling	No
Picture Alignment	Center
Picture Type	Embedded
Picture Size Mode	Clip
Width	12.335cm
Auto Center	No
Auto Resize	Yes
Fit to Screen	Yes
Border Style	Sizable
Record Selectors	Yes
Navigation Buttons	Yes
Navigation Caption	
Dividing Lines	No

Fig. 8.12 Property Sheet

All of these open the Property Sheet which replaces the Field List pane if it was open. You can't have them both open at the same time. It is dockable, so you can drag its title bar and position it where you like on the screen. This makes it very easy to get it out of your working area.

As shown in Fig. 8.12 it is made up of five tabbed pages, and lists all of the characteristics associated with the selected object or control. You can change any of the properties to control exactly how an object looks and functions.

If a down-arrow appears when you click in the property box to the right of a property, it will list the available options for you to select. Otherwise you can just type in a value. Sometimes you can press **Shift+F2** to open the Zoom box we saw before which is useful for entering or viewing long values.

As you get more familiar with Access you will find yourself using the Property Sheets more and more.

The Build Button

With some Properties, a window, dialogue box, or wizard is available to help you create the property settings. When such help is available (as with the top Property shown in Fig. 8.12) Access displays a small button with an ellipsis [...] next to the property box; this is the **Build** button. If you click the Build button, Access opens the appropriate window, dialogue box, or wizard for you to make your choices.

The Form Area

You may have noticed that in Fig. 8.11 our new form displays without a tab and is in a window of its own.

Overlapping Windows

To overlap windows, click the **Office Button** [icon], **Access Options** and select the Current Database sheet. In the **Document Window Options** section of the right pane click the **Overlapping Windows** radio button pointed to in Fig. 8.13 below, then click **OK**. On the message box that appears, click **OK** and close and reopen the database.

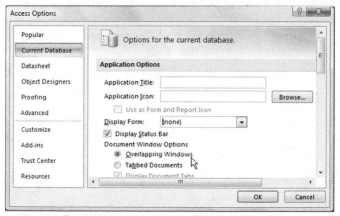

Fig. 8.13 Access Document Window Options

With overlapping windows, Access forms, tables and reports appear as regular windows within the main Access window. They have their own system buttons _ ⊡ ✕ like any other Windows window, but are still opened by double-clicking their entry in the Navigation Pane. With overlapping windows set, the database title no longer appears in the title bar of the Access window.

Form Header and Footer Areas

When a form is first opened in Design View it contains a **Form Selection** button ▪, two rulers, two scroll bars, a horizontal bar labelled Detail, and a working area with a grid. Some of these can be toggled on and off from buttons in the **Arrange**, **Show/Hide** group, shown here.

As well as the Detail section to hold its working controls, a form can have Header and Footer sections to display titles and other information. To add these, either right-click in the form and select **Form Header/Footer**, or click the **Arrange**, **Show/Hide**, **Form Header/Footer** button on the Ribbon.

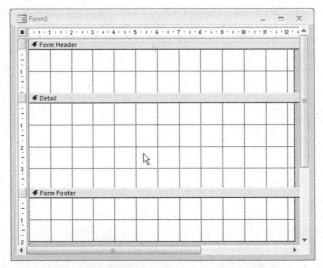

Fig. 8.14 A Blank Form with Header and Footer Areas

If you don't want the Footer area, you can reduce it completely by dragging its bottom up to the Footer bar. When a form is created with the Form Wizard, both the header and the footer sections are added but the footer section is completely reduced in this way.

The Design Controls

The **Design**, **Controls** in Design View can be used either to design a Form or Report from scratch, or to add controls to existing ones. The main controls are shown in Fig. 8.15 below and described on the following pages.

Fig. 8.15 Access 2007's Design Tools

At the left end of the Controls group are four self-explanatory tools to add a **Logo** or picture, a **Title**, **Page Numbers**, or the **Date and Time** to the Header area. You can then move them to wherever you want on the form.

 Text Box

Text boxes are used to display data from a record. They are then said to be bound as they are directly linked to the field data. They can also be unbound, or not linked to field data, say to display the results of a calculation or to accept input.

Aa **Label**

You use labels on a form or report to display text such as titles or captions. Labels do not display values from fields, are always unbound and they stay the same between records.

Button

You use a command button on a form to start a macro to implement an action or a set of actions. The macro, or event procedure, must be attached to the button's **On Click** property. You can create around thirty different types of - command buttons with the Command Button Wizard.

 Combo Box

A combo box is like a text box and a list box combined. When you enter text or select a value in a bound combo box the entered or selected value is inserted into the field that the combo box is bound to. On a form, you can use a combo box instead of a list box; it takes up less room, and you can type new values in it, as well as select values from a list.

 List Box

It is often quicker and easier to select a value from a list than to remember it and then type it into a form field. A list box gives this facility, and providing a fixed list of choices also helps prevent simple typing errors. In a form, a list box can have one or more columns. If a multiple-column list box is bound, Access stores the values from one of the columns.

 Subform/Subreport

A subform is a form within a form and a subreport is a report within a report, the primary form or report being the main one, and the other the 'sub' one. These are especially effective when you want to show data from tables or queries with a one-to-many relationship, as we have seen in our example a few pages back.

 Line

Draws a line on a form or report. Click anywhere on the form and drag to create the line. To make small adjustments to the length or angle of a line, select it, hold down the **Shift** key, and press one of the arrow keys.

Fig. 8.16 Line
Thickness and
Type Options

To make small adjustments in the placement of a line, hold down the **Ctrl** key and press one of the arrow keys. To change the thickness of a line, select it, click the arrow next to the **Design**, **Controls**, **Line Thickness** button and then select the line thickness you want.

To change the line style to dots, dashes, etc., click the arrow next to the **Design**, **Controls**, **Line Type** button and select the style you want. To change the colour of the line use the **Design**, **Controls**, **Line Color** button.

 Rectangle
Draws an 'empty' rectangle on a form or report. You can change the colour, line thickness and line type with the **Line Color**, **Line Thickness** and **Line Type** buttons, as above.

 Bound Object Frame
These are used to display bound OLE objects (images or spreadsheet tables for example) that are actually stored in a table in the database. Double-clicking the object will then open the application that was used to create it so that you can edit it in-situ.

 Option Group
In a form or report, an option group consists of a group frame with a set of check boxes, option buttons, or toggle buttons. It is used to display a limited set of alternatives where only one can be selected at a time. An option group makes selecting a value easy because you can just click the value that you want.

 Check Box
You can use a check box on a form or report as a stand-alone control to display a Yes/No value from an underlying table, query, or SQL statement. If the box contains a check mark, the value is Yes; if it doesn't, the value is No.

Option Button

You can use option buttons in three main ways:

- as a stand-alone control to display a Yes/No value from an underlying record source,

- in an option group to display values to choose from,

- in a custom dialogue box to accept user input.

With the first two uses the option buttons would be bound, and in the last unbound.

 Toggle Button

A toggle button on a form is used to change the state of a field, for example to display a Yes/No, True/False, or On/Off value from an underlying record source. When you click a toggle button that is, say, bound to a Yes/No field in a database, the value in the underlying table displays according to the field's Yes/No property. You can place pictures on toggle buttons.

 Tab Control

This can be used to present several pages of information as a single set on a form. Each page is given a headed tab and it is accessed by clicking on this tab.

Fig. 8.17 A Tab Control

 Insert Page

This control becomes active when you select a tab of an existing Tab Control on a form. When clicked, it inserts a new tabbed page in the Tab Control.

 Insert Chart

Opens the Chart Wizard to help you create a chart, or graph, from your data and then inserts it on the form or report.

Unbound Object Frame

Unbound object frames can be used to add unbound images (or other objects like spreadsheet tables) to a form or report when you may want to be able to edit them directly from the form or report. Double-clicking the image will then open the application that was used to create it so that you can edit it in-situ. The image is slower to load than with Image controls though.

 Image

The image control is used to add unbound images, or pictures, to a form, as long as you will not need to edit them in the future. The images can be embedded in the database itself, which makes them very fast to load, or linked, which trims the database size. This is controlled by the **Picture Type** property.

 Insert or Remove Page Break

The Page Break tool lets you design multiple screen (or page) forms. Remember to place page breaks above, or below, other controls to avoid splitting their data.

 Insert Hyperlink

This control holds links to Web pages, pictures, an e-mail address or other programs. Clicking the link on the form will jump the user to the linked page or application.

 Attachment

Lets you view attachments in a form or report as long as the control is bound to a field in a table set to the Attachments data type. Image files are rendered automatically and other types of attached files show as icons.

 Insert ActiveX Control

On our PCs this button opens lists of many other control types to use. Some of these may require extra software to be installed, but it is well worth experimenting here.

Like the three 'Line' buttons described earlier, the other buttons in the right section of the **Controls** group do not create controls, but help you with the design process.

 Select

Change to the selection cursor ⌖ from one of the other control cursors. If you clicked a control but don't want to use it any more, you can click the Select button to return to the normal selection cursor.

 Select All

Select all the controls on the Form or Report in Design View.

 Use Control Wizards

This is a toggle button which 'lights up' when selected (the default). With some of the Controls, Access will then open a Wizard to help you make choices when placing the Control. Unless you really know what you are doing, it is as well to keep this selection active.

 Set Control Defaults

Use this button to set the Property selections for the active control as the defaults for that control type. Useful when you want to create more controls with the same properties, but you should use this button with care.

 Special Effect

This button lets you quickly set the **Special Effect** Property of selected objects on the form or report. Clicking its down-arrow opens the list of six options for improving the visual display of controls. We seem to use the **Sunken** effect most of the time.

Fig. 8.18

To see these effects at their best you usually need to set suitable colours for your controls and the Form itself. This is easiest done by right-clicking the object and selecting from the **Fill/Back Color** picker.

A Design Procedure

To create a new form from scratch, you could use the following procedure.

- Click the **Create**, **Forms**, **Form Design** button to create a new blank form and switch to Design View.

- Decide what fields you want included, and drag them from the Field List pane (page 135). This will also add labels for the controls.

- If necessary, edit the labels with the **Format**, **Font** options.

- Arrange the controls on the form by dragging them around the form and set suitable Control Layouts (page 132).

- Create a Header on the form and add a title and maybe a logo to it (page 139).

- Add any other controls you want by clicking their buttons in the **Design**, **Controls** group and then dragging the pointer on a blank area of form. When the mouse button is released the new control will be set.

- In the Property Sheet of each control (page 136) set its properties so that it looks and functions as you want.

AutoFormat

An easy way to change the format of an entire form is to use one of the AutoFormats included with Access 2007. You can use an AutoFormat as it is out of the box, or you can choose to apply certain parts of it.

Open the form you want to format in Design View, click the **Arrange**, **AutoFormat**, **AutoFormat** button, shown here, and select the format you want to apply from the gallery of options that opens, shown in Fig. 8.19.

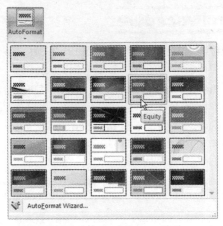

Fig. 8.19 Autoformat Gallery Options

It is worth experimenting with this feature, you may find a form format that fits your database completely. Clicking an option in the gallery applies that format to the whole form that is active.

To Autoformat only parts of your form, click **AutoFormat Wizard** and then the **Options >>** button. You can then select which **Attributes to Apply** by selecting the **Font**, **Color** or **Border** check boxes which appear at the bottom of the wizard box.

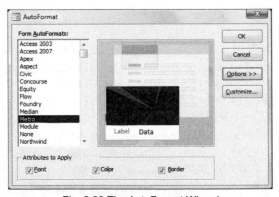

Fig. 8.20 The AutoFormat Wizard

A Customised Form

We have played around with our Customer Invoice Details form in Design View, as can be seen in Fig. 8.21 below. You should not have too much trouble now with most of the changes. The title is formatted text inside a Label control and several of the Text Boxes have been re-sized and moved, or even deleted!

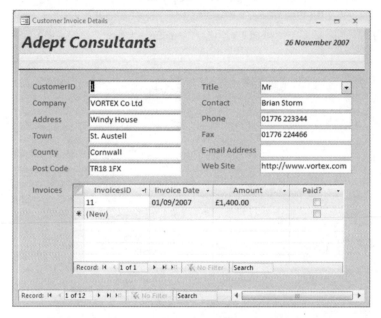

Fig. 8.21 Our Customer Invoice Details Form Ready For Use

If you are interested, the vertical bar at the left of the form was removed by setting the **Record Selectors** Property of the Form to **No**.

To get the 3-dimensional effect in the main section of the form, we set the **Back Color** property of Detail to a mid-grey from the colour picker, and the **Special Effect** property of all the control data boxes to **Sunken**.

The Totals Row

You may have noticed that Access 2007 has a new feature which lets you add a Totals row to tables and queries that are open in Datasheet View. This simplifies the process of summing columns of data, or creating averages, counting the number of items in a column, and finding the minimum or maximum value in a column of data.

It also means you don't always need to put controls on your forms and reports to carry out these functions.

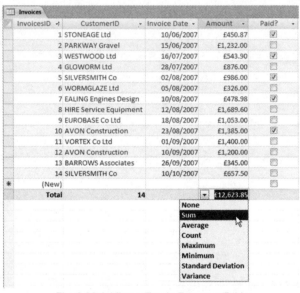

Fig. 8.22 Adding a Totals Row to a Table

To add a Totals row to a table, click the **Home**, **Records**, **Totals** button Σ Totals. A new Total row will be placed below the star ＊ row, as shown in Fig. 8.22 above. In the Total row, click the field that you want to sum, and then select **SUM** from the drop-down list. The **Count** function counts the number of items in a column and works with all data types.

You can't cut or delete a Totals row, you turn it on or off with the Σ Totals button.

9

Using Reports

In Access, a report is an effective way to present data in printed format. The data in a report is taken from a database table or query, and the other report information is stored in the report's design. This is shown graphically in Fig. 9.1 below, which was part of an Access Help page.

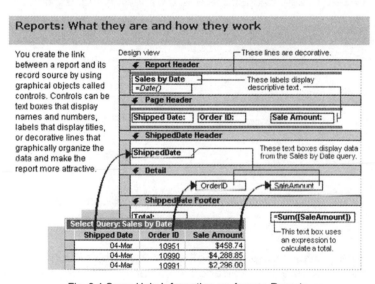

Fig. 9.1 Some Help Information on Access Reports

When designing a report you can combine data from any of the tables, or queries, of your database. As with a form, you do this in either Layout or Design View by adding fields and controls to the design grid. These controls define the source of the information in the database, and its printed appearance.

The Report Wizard

To see how easy it can be, we will use the skills gained in manipulating Access forms in Design View to produce a very quick, but acceptable report using the Report Wizard. In our example database, **Adept Consultants**, we will produce a report based on the Unpaid Invoices query.

 The controls for creating reports are located in the **Create**, **Reports** group, as shown here. As you can see, there are several different options available for you to choose from. For now click the **Create**, **Reports**, **Report Wizard** button, to open the window shown in Fig. 9.2 below.

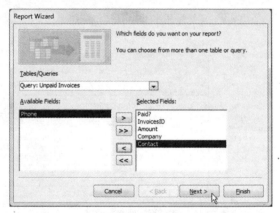

Fig. 9.2 The Report Wizard Opening Window

Select **Query: Unpaid Invoices** in the **Tables/Queries** box as the source for the report data, and move all the fields except Paid? to the **Selected Fields** box to appear on your report. Select to view data **by Invoices**, the InvoicesID field as the sort field and **Tabular** as the **Layout** and accept all other default settings. In the last box give it the title Unpaid Invoices Report, select **Preview the report** and click **Finish**.

The report is quickly created for you as a Print Preview, shown in Fig. 9.3 on the next page, but the format leaves something to be desired.

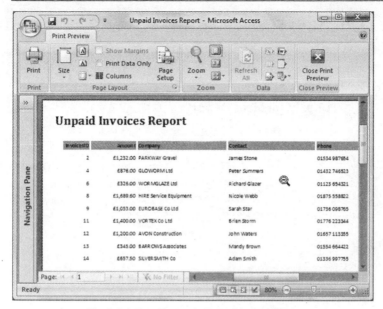

Fig. 9.3 A Raw Report in Print Preview Mode

The problem is that the field lengths are wrong, they are too close together with the text fields being left justified and the numerical fields right justified.

These problems are most easily corrected in Layout View, opened by clicking the **Layout View** button on the status bar. This is similar to the Layout View we used for Forms in the last chapter. As you can see in Fig. 9.4 it adds three new tabs to the Ribbon, **Format**, **Arrange** and **Page Setup**.

We selected each column in turn by clicking its header and dragged the right side to shorten the field length, as shown in Fig. 9.4. This is easy to do in Layout View as the report has a Tabular Control Layout. Remember our form data in the last chapter had a Stacked Control Layout.

Next we clicked the brown ⊞ button above the data, to select all the report data, clicked the **Arrange**, **Control Layout**, **Control Padding** button shown here and selected **Medium** from the list. This added more space between the columns.

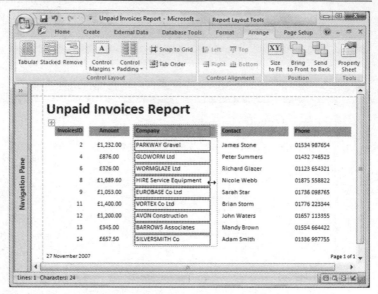

Fig. 9.4 Improving the Report in Layout View

To centre justify the Amount column, as shown above, we selected the column by clicking in its header and clicked the **Home**, **Font**, **Center** button ≣. We also selected the title and changed its Font settings in the **Home**, **Font** group.

The report now looks a lot better, as can be seen in Print Preview mode in Fig. 9.5 below.

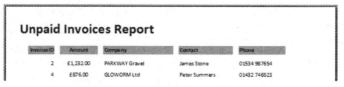

Fig. 9.5 Print Preview of the Corrected Report Layout

It doesn't take much tweaking to get good results, and of course you only need to do this once, as long as you save your changes. The next time you double-click the name of this report in the Navigation Pane, it will be produced again with the most up-to-date data.

Types of Access Reports

In Design View you can, if you have the skill and time, create reports completely on your own. Initially we are sure most people will be happy using one of the Wizards to create their reports, and then spend a few minutes (hopefully not hours) getting the final result. The report creating options are:

Report Wizard – Automatically creates Columnar, Tabular or Justified reports based on fields and options you select. We used the Tabular one earlier.

Report – Automatically produces a tabular report with just one click.

Blank Report – Opens a new empty report in Layout View and opens the Fields List for you to select from.

Form Design – Opens a new blank report in Design View.

Label Wizard – creates a report formatted for you to print on mailing labels.

When you action the **Report** option above, from a table or query, Access uses all the fields from that source to create a report. With the Report Wizard, however, you can select fields from more than one table or query source. How you start your reports is up to you. You may find the **Report** option easier, once you get used to it.

Report Views

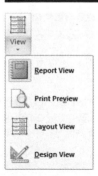

With Access 2007 there are four possible screen views of a report, accessed either from the menu opened by clicking the down-arrow below the **Home**, **Views**, **View** button, shown here, or by clicking one of the **Views** buttons on the Status bar.

Fig. 9.6 The Access 2007 Report Views

Report View

This view simply shows what the report will look like on paper. You can't actually make any changes to the report though as it is in read-only mode.

Layout View

This is the easiest view for making report changes, and will probably provide most of the tools you will need for finishing your reports. You can adjust column widths, rearrange columns, and add or modify grouping levels and totals. You can drag new fields from the Fields List to the report design and set the properties for the report and its controls. For all these operations you can actually see your data while you are making changes to the report format.

Design View

If you can't make the changes you want in Layout View, you will have to try Design View. This view shows the underlying structure of the report, and as with forms, provides more design tools than Layout View. You can place the same controls on the report as you can on a form, and you can adjust the alignment of controls more precisely.

Print Preview

This view shows the report on the screen as it will be printed with all its data, which could save a few trees and equally important to you, a lot of frustration, ink and wear and tear on your printer!

The Print Preview window, shown in Fig. 9.3, has its own Ribbon with **Page Layout** options, **Zoom** viewing options for magnification and to control the number of report pages actually shown. The pointer is set as a magnifier and there is a Zoom Slider on the Status bar.

To print the document to paper click the **Print** button, and to other file formats click a button in the **Data** group. To return to your working report, click the **Close Print Preview** button. This is a very powerful facility.

Help on Report Building

The reporting section of Access 2007 is even more powerful than previous versions of the package, and we only have space to give a flavour of it here. We suggest you spend an hour or two in the Help section of Access, opened as usual with the **F1** key, or by clicking the **Microsoft Office Access Help** button in the top right of the Access screen.

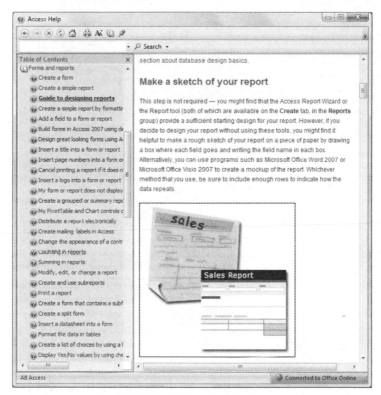

Fig. 9.7 Getting Help on Building Reports

Some of the Help sections are quite detailed and easy to understand, as in the example shown here.

The Northwind Database

The other main source of inspiration on reports, and other database components, are the Templates offered in Access's Get Started window we saw in Fig. 3.3 on page 36. Templates are professionally pre-built databases that you can download, open and use right away.

Fig. 9.8 Downloading the Northwind 2007 Database

For us, clicking the **Sample** option in **Template Categories** gave us access to the Northwind 2007 sample database, as shown above in Fig. 9.8. Hopefully you will have the same option. Clicking the **Download** button will save it to your PC. If you don't like the saving path offered you can click the browse button 📂 and change it.

Open this database and have a good look at it. Don't worry about its complexity, but it is a good example of what can be done with Access. It even includes some data for you to play with!

In the Navigation Pane browse through the reports which look at the data (15 in our case, but you may have a different version). We show a sample from the Monthly Sales Report in Report View in Fig. 9.9 below, and show it in Design View in Fig. 9.10 on the next page, so that you can compare them and get some idea how the final report is made up.

Fig. 9.9 A Report from the Northwind 2007 Sample Database

The data is a little dated, but it is the design we are looking at! We shall see that the report has a grouping selection, based on the Month.

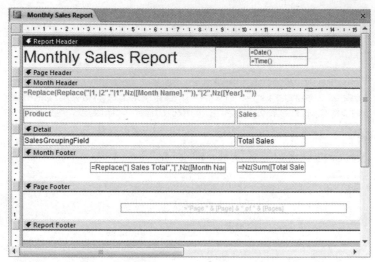

Fig. 9.10 The Northwind Report in Design View

There are seven bands shown above in this report and what prints in each band of the final report depends on the controls (mainly Labels and Text Boxes) placed on it. The function of each band and where its output appears is shown below (in our example above the Group is Month):

Report Header – appears at the start of a report

> **Page Header** – appears at the top of each report page

>> **Group Header** – appears above a new group

>>> **Report Detail** – the main body of report data

>> **Group Footer** – appears at the end of a group

> **Page Footer** – appears at the bottom of each page

Report Footer – appears at the end of a report.

Typically the report header is used for the report title, a logo and maybe the current date, and the report footer for report totals, such as sums, counts and averages. Page headers and footers are used for report titles and page numbers. A group header would show the field that is being grouped on, and a group footer would show group totals.

Sorting and Grouping Records

A group is a collection of records, along with any introductory and summary information displayed with the records. A group consists of a group header, nested groups (if any), detail records, and a group footer. In the previous example there was only one report group, but you can sort and group on up to 10 fields or expressions in a report. You control this with the report open in Design View, by clicking the **Design**, **Grouping & Totals**, **Group & Sort** button. This opens the Group, Sort, and Total pane, shown below.

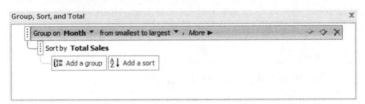

Fig. 9.11 The Group Sort and Total Pane

For our example, as you can see above, the report is grouped on Month and sorted by Total Sales. To add a new sorting or grouping level, click in the **Add a group** or **Add a sort** boxes.

A new line is added to the Group, Sort, and Total pane, and a list of available fields is displayed, as shown in Fig. 9.12.

The field names will depend on the data in your database. You can click one of them or click **expression** below the list of fields to enter an expression in the expression builder that opens.

Fig. 9.12 Adding a New Sort or Group

Once you choose a field or enter an expression, Access adds the grouping level to the report. If you are in Layout View, the display changes immediately to show the new changes. For more detail here we suggest you look at the **Create a grouped or summary report** entry in the Help system.

Creating a Calculated Control

It is often very useful to have a report calculate values from the data extracted from the database, such as totals, averages, percentages, etc. To describe how to do this, we will place a total value on the Unpaid Invoices Report we designed at the beginning of the chapter.

Open the Unpaid Invoices Report of the Adept Consultants database in Design View and drag the Report Footer down to make room for the new controls. Click the **Design**, **Controls**, **Text Box** tool button ⓐⓑⓛ on the Ribbon and 'drag' a new box about the same size as and below the Amount control in the Detail band, as shown in Fig. 9.13.

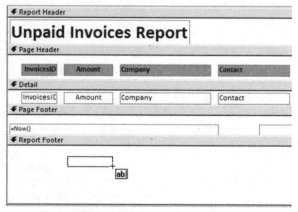

Fig. 9.13 Placing a Text Box Control in a Report

Now, in the same way, place a Label to the left of the Text Box and type 'Total Value' in the Label. If necessary, re-size the boxes as shown in Fig. 9.14 on the facing page.

We must now enter the Expression into the Text box to carry out the required calculation. Make sure the Text Box control is selected, right-click in it and select **Properties** to display the control's property sheet. Click the All tab, as shown in Fig. 9.14 and type the new control name 'Total' in the **Name** property box.

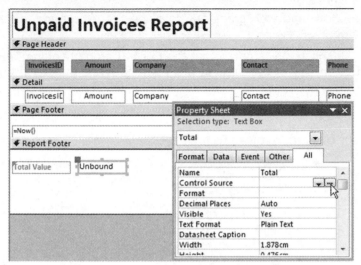

Fig. 9.14 Setting the Text Box Control Source Property

Click the **Control Source** property box to select it and click the **Build** button ••• pointed to above. This opens the Expression Builder, shown in Fig. 9.15 below.

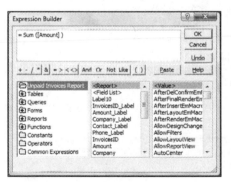

In fact with a text box, you can type the expression directly into it, but we wanted to introduce the Expression Builder again.

To read more about this feature we suggest you go back to page 103.

Fig. 9.15 The Expression Builder

The expression you need to total the Amount field is:

```
=Sum([Amount])
```

Either type this into the Expression Builder, or experiment with the builder until you have this expression in the top window, and then press **OK** to place the expression in the properties sheet.

It only remains now to set the **Format** property of the Text Box to **Currency**. Clicking the **Print Preview** button on the Status bar should now show something like the following.

Unpaid Invoices Report

InvoicesID	Amount	Company	Contact	Phone
2	£1,232.00	PARKWAY Gravel	James Stone	01534 987654
4	£876.00	GLOWORM Ltd	Peter Summers	01432 746523
6	£326.00	WORMGLAZE Ltd	Richard Glazer	01123 654321
8	£1,689.60	HIRE Service Equipment	Nicole Webb	01875 558822
9	£1,053.00	EUROBASE Co Ltd	Sarah Star	01736 098765
11	£1,400.00	VORTEX Co Ltd	Brian Storm	01776 223344
12	£1,200.00	AVON Construction	John Waters	01657 113355
13	£345.00	BARROWS Associates	Mandy Brown	01554 664422
14	£657.50	SILVERSMITH Co	Adam Smith	01336 997755
Total Value	£8,779.10			

Fig. 9.16 Print Preview of the Modified Report

In a calculated control you should always start each expression with the = operator as can be seen on the next page where we list the other arithmetic expressions you can use in an Access 2007 database report or form.

It is usually easier to type the expression straight into a text box, or a property box, and don't forget that if you need more room to type the expression in the box, the **Shift+F2** keystroke combination will open the Zoom box for you.

Arithmetic Expressions

Expression	*Description*
=Avg([Field])	Uses the Avg function to display the average of the values of the 'Field' control.
=Count([Field])	Uses the Count function to display the number of records in the 'Field' control.
=Sum([Field])	Uses the Sum function to display the sum of the values of the 'Field' control.
=Sum([Field1]*[Field2])	Uses the Sum function to display the sum of the product of the values of the 'Field1' and 'Field2' controls.
=[Sales]/Sum([Sales])	Displays the percentage of sales, determined by dividing the value of the Sales control by the sum of all the values of the Sales control. The control's Format property must be set to Percent for this to work.

Access has quite an extensive list of expressions that can be used in tables and forms. Amongst other things, these can be used to handle text, numbers, dates, page numbers and control values.

To find out more on these, type 'expressions' in the **Search** box of Access Help, and press the **Enter** key. This will show links to a range of useful pages of help.

Printing a Report

Print

Printing a report to paper in Access is best done with it open in the Print Preview window (see page 154). If necessary, first use the **Page Layout** commands to set the paper size, orientation and margin settings. When you are ready, click the **Print** button to open the Print dialogue box shown below in Fig. 9.17.

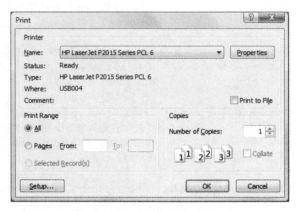

Fig. 9.17 The Print Dialogue Box

The settings in the Print dialogue box allow you to select the number of copies, and which pages, you want printed. You can change the printer by clicking the down arrow against the **Name** box which displays the printers on your system.

Clicking the **Properties** and **Setup** buttons gives you access to some more advanced print options, and gives you another chance to select the paper size, orientation, etc.

Clicking the **OK** button on these various multilevel dialogue boxes, accepts your selections and returns you to the previous level dialogue box, until the Print dialogue box is reached. Selecting **OK** here, sends your report either to the printer connected to your computer or to a network. Selecting **Cancel** on any level dialogue box, aborts the selections made at that level.

10

Working with Data

In this chapter we discuss several aspects of working with data; masking, importing or linking data, attaching pictures, hypertext links and sharing your data. The first of these is useful for restricting data input into an Access field, such as a postcode or telephone number.

The Input Mask Property

You can use the **Input Mask** property to make data entry easier and control the values you enter in a text box. For example, you could create an input mask for a Post Code field that shows you exactly how to enter a new postcode.

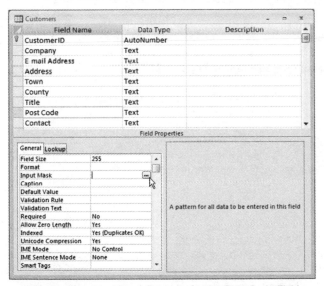

Fig. 10.1 The Input Mask Property for the Post Code Field

To place an input mask, open the **Adept Consultants** database, select the Customers table, press the **Design View** button, and select the Post Code field. Clicking in the **Input Mask** field in the **Field Properties** section, shown in Fig. 10.1 on the previous page, shows a **Build** button ⋯ at the extreme right of the field. When clicked this opens the Input Mask Wizard, shown in Fig. 10.2 below.

Fig. 10.2 The Input Mask Wizard

Select Postal Code from the **Input Mask** list, and press **Next** to display the second dialogue box (Fig. 10.3) in which you can edit the default Input Mask. You can also type variations of the postcode in the **Try It** box.

Fig. 10.3 Adding an Input Mask with the Wizard

Clicking the **Finish** button will place the mask in the Field Properties box and display the **Property Update Options** button shown below.

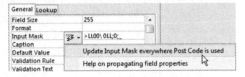

Fig. 10.4 The Property Update Options Button

This gives you the option to place the new Input Mask in the Post Code fields of all your Access tables. Very useful!

Password Masks

If you want to create a password-entry control, you use the Password input mask to set the **Input Mask** property to the word 'Password'. This then displays an asterisk (*) on the screen for every character typed into that field.

Only characters that you type directly in a control or combo box are affected by the input mask. Access ignores any input masks when you import data, or run an action query.

Input Mask Characters

The **Input Mask** property can contain up to three sections separated by semicolons (;). Within each section a certain number of characters are allowed. These characters and their description are listed below.

Character	*Description*
0	Signifies a digit (0 to 9); entry required. The plus (+) and minus (–) signs are not allowed.
9	Signifies a digit or space; entry not required. The plus and minus signs are not allowed.

#	Signifies a digit or space; entry not required, spaces are displayed as blanks while in Edit mode, but blanks are removed when data is saved. The plus and minus signs are allowed.
L	Signifies a letter (A to Z); entry required.
?	Signifies a letter (A to Z); entry optional.
A	Signifies a letter or digit; entry required.
a	Signifies a letter or digit; entry optional.
&	Signifies any character or a space; entry required.
C	Signifies any character or a space; entry optional.
. , : ; – /	Signifies a decimal placeholder and thousand, date, and time separators. (The actual character used depends on the settings in the Regional Settings section of the Windows Control Panel).
<	Causes all characters to be converted to lowercase.
>	Causes all characters to be converted to uppercase.
!	Causes the input mask to display from right to left, rather than from left to right, when characters on the left side of the input mask are optional. Characters typed into the mask always fill it from left to right. You can include the exclamation point anywhere in the input mask.
\	Causes the character that follows to be displayed as the literal character (for example, \A is displayed as just A).

Thus, we can interpret the postcode mask shown in Fig. 10.4 as follows:

> \>   Convert all characters entered to upper case.
> **L**   Letter (A-Z) expected; entry required.
> **L**   Letter (A-Z) expected; entry required.
> **0**   Digit (0-9) expected; entry required.
> **0**   Digit (0-9) expected; entry required.
> \\   Cause character following backslash (in this case a space) to appear as such
> **0**   Digit (0-9) expected; entry required.
> **L**   Letter (A-Z) expected; entry required.
> **L**   Letter (A-Z) expected; entry required.

However, this postcode (two letters followed by two numbers, then a space followed by one number, then two letters, will not be adequate for all postcode variations encountered in the UK.

For example, some codes have only one number following the first two letters, like CB1 2PU, others particularly in London have only one leading letter, like N1 0RD, while if you write to the BBC you will need the W1A 1AA code.

A postcode mask suitable for most eventualities in the UK could be:

>LAaaaaaa

We will leave it to you to experiment further with input masks. They can be useful for phone number and date fields as well.

Importing Data into Access

In this book so far we have discussed designing tables and entering data manually into them, but to make your life easier, Access 2007 can import existing data from a range of different sources.

Pasting into an Access Table

If your data is has been created or stored in a spreadsheet program, such as Excel 2007, it will be separated into columns, and should be easy to copy straight to Access.

	A	B	C	D	E	F	G
1	Name	Composition	Hardness	Colour	Density	Streak	
2	Talc	Mg3Si4O10(OH)2	1	White	2.75	White	
3	Gypsum	CaSO4·2H2O	2	White	2.3	White	
4	Calcite	CaCO3	3	Colourless	2.71	White	
5	Fluorite	CaF2	4	White - green	3.13	White	
6	Apatite	Ca5(PO4)3(OH,Cl,F)	5	Green	3.84	White	
7	Orthoclase	KAlSi3O8	6	Colourless	2.56	White	
8	Quartz	SiO2	7	Colourless	2.62	White	
9	Topaz	Al2SiO4(OH,F)2	8	Pale yellow	3.55	White	
10	Corundum	Al2O3	9	Blue - gray	4.05	None	
11	Diamond	C (pure carbon)	10	Colourless	3.51	Colourless	
12							

Fig. 10.5 Part of an Excel Worksheet Selected for Copying

In Excel you simply select the data you want to transfer to Access, including the column labels, as shown in Fig. 10.5 above. Then click the **Home**, **Clipboard**, **Copy** button (or **Ctrl+C**) to copy the range to the clipboard.

In the Access database where you want the data, click the **Create**, **Table** button to open a new table and click the **Home**, **Clipboard**, **Paste** button (or **Ctrl+V**), to paste the data into the new table, as shown in Fig. 10.6. You will be asked to confirm the action, just click **Yes** to proceed.

When you paste data into an empty table, Access sets the data type of each field according to what kind of data it finds there. If a pasted field contains nothing but date values, Access applies the Date/Time data type to that field. If the pasted field contains only the words "yes" and "no", Access would apply the Yes/No data type to the field.

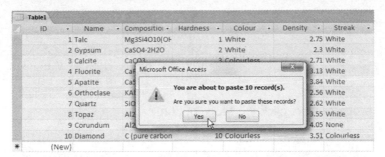

Fig. 10.6 Excel Data Pasted into a New Access Table

As shown in our example, Access names the fields depending on what it finds in the first row of pasted data. If the first row is similar in type to the rows that follow, Access assumes it is part of the data and gives generic names, such as F1, F2, etc., to the fields. You should then rename these as soon as possible. If the first row of pasted data is not similar to the rows that follow, Access assumes that it contains field names, as has happened in Fig. 10.6.

Importing Data

Access makes it easy to import data from other programs, such as:

Other Access databases
Excel spreadsheets
Microsoft Windows SharePoint Services
Text files
XML files
ODBC databases
HTML documents
Microsoft Office Outlook
dBase
Paradox
Lotus 1-2-3

You will find these options on the **Import** group of the External Data tab, shown here. Clicking any of them opens the Get External Data dialogue box. If you don't see the correct program type, click the **More** button.

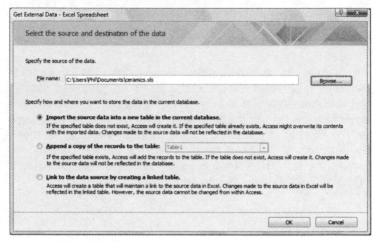

Fig. 10.7 The Get External Data Dialogue Box

In the Get External Data dialogue box, click the **Browse** button and locate the source data file. Click the option that you want under **Specify how and where you want to store the data in the current database**.

As can be seen, you can create a new table for the imported data, append the data to an existing table, or create a linked table that maintains a link to the data source. Clicking the **OK** button starts the Import Wizard.

The Wizard procedure depends on the options chosen, so just follow the instructions given and on the last page click the **Finish** button.

If you can't find the correct format type in the **Import** group, you may need to save the data in a common file format before you can import it into Access.

The Table Analyzer Wizard

After your data has been imported into an Access table, if it is fairly complex, you can click the **Database Tools**, **Analyze**, **Analyze Table** button 🔁 Analyze Table and use the Table Analyzer Wizard to show you repeating data. The wizard then recommends how to organise your imported data into separate tables, so that it is stored in the most efficient way.

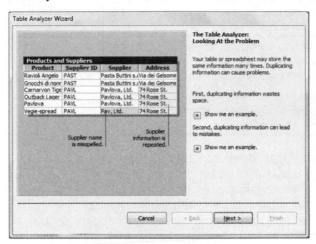

Fig. 10.8 The Table Analyzer Wizard

Importing or Linking Data

The list on page 171 shows which types of data from other programs Access can import or link to.

Importing data creates a copy of the information in a new table in your current Access database; the source table or file is not altered. Linking data allows you to read and update data in the external data source without importing; the external data source's format is not altered so that you can continue to use the file with the program that created it originally, and you can also add, delete, or edit such data using Access.

In general, you import or link information depending on the imposed situation, as follows:

Imposed Situation	*Method to Adopt*
Inserted data needs to be updated in Access as changes are made to the data in the source file, or Source file will always be available and you want to minimise the size of the Access data file.	Link
Inserted information might need to be updated but source file might not be always accessible, or Access data file needs to be edited without having these changes reflected in the source file.	Import

Access uses different icons to represent linked tables and tables that are stored in the current database, as shown here. The icon that represents a linked table remains in the Navigation Pane along with tables in the current database, so you can open the table whenever you want.

```
◆dB EMPLOYEE — dBASE
◆Px Products    — Paradox
◆▦ Suppliers    — Access
```

Access displays a different icon for tables from each type of source database. If you delete the icon for a linked table, you delete the link from Access to the table, but not the external table itself.

When importing data, you cannot append it to existing tables (except when importing spreadsheet or text files). However, once you have imported a table, you can use an append query to add its data to another table.

Images in Access

With version 2007 of Access you can now store images in your database. Previous versions used OLE to show images, whereas Access 2007 stores attached image files in their native formats, and you do not need to install additional software to view the images.

Access 2007 uses 'Attachments' to do this, which can store several files in a single field. You can even store different types of files in the same field. Our Adept example database, for example, could store several photographs, a Word document and an Excel spreadsheet in one field.

Supported File Formats

Access 2007 supports the following graphic file formats, and renders them without the need for additional software.

.bmp	Windows Bitmap
.rle	Run Length Encoded Bitmap
.dib	Device Independent Bitmap
.gif	Graphics Interchange Format
.jpeg, .jpg, .jpe	Joint Photographic Experts Group
.exif	Exchangeable File Format
.png	Portable Network Graphics
.tiff, .tif	Tagged Image File Format
.icon, .ico	Icon
.wmf	Windows Metafile
.emf	Enhanced Metafile.

The other file formats you can save as attachments are:

.log	Log files
.text, .txt	Text files
.zip	compressed files

Microsoft Office 2007 program files.

Adding an Attachment Field

To use attachments in Access 2007, you must first add an attachment field to at least one of the tables in your database. With the table open in Datasheet View, click the first available blank column with the **Add New Field** column header.

Click the down arrow next to the **Datasheet**, **Data Type & Formatting**, **Data Type** button and select **Attachment**. Access sets the data type for the field to Attachment, and places a paper clip icon 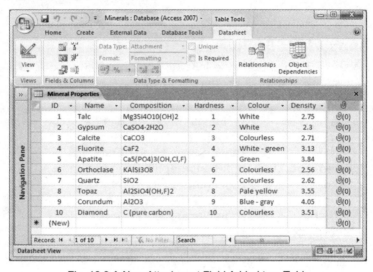 in the header row of the field, and a ⓪(0) symbol in every field cell of the table, as shown in our example Fig. 10.9 below.

Fig. 10.9 A New Attachment Field Added to a Table

Here we have created a table of mineral properties and are adding an Attachment field to hold photographs of each mineral.

There are two things to remember with Attachment fields, you can't normally enter text in the field header, and you can't convert an Attachment field to another data type – you can only delete it.

Attaching Files

To add files to the Attachment field in Datasheet View, double-click the Attachment field cell to hold the file(s) and open the Attachments dialogue box, shown in Fig. 10.10.

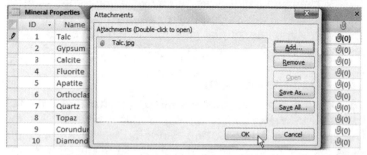

Fig. 10.10 Adding an Attachment File to a Table Cell

Clicking the **Add** button opens the Windows Choose File dialogue box. Use the **Look in** list to navigate to the file or files that you want to attach to the record, and click **Open**. You can select multiple files of any supported data type. Click **OK** to add the files to your table.

When we did this as above, the icon in the Attachment field cell of the Talc record changed from ⬛(0) to ⬛(1), to show that the cell had one file attached to it, (Talc.jpg).

The only way to access or see attached pictures in a Table is to double-click the ⬛(1) icon to open the Attachments box shown above, and double-click the file you want to view in the list. With us, this opens image files in the Windows Photo Gallery, but your setup may be different.

The usual way to use attached picture files is to set up a form or report so that they show automatically whenever the form or report is opened.

Attachments in Forms and Reports

 To use attachments with a form or report you use the Attachment control (page 143) which renders image files automatically as you move among your records. The control also allows you to browse any attached files and open the Attachments dialogue box in which you can add, remove, edit, and save attachments from a form.

The Attachment Control

To add an Attachment control to an open form or report, click the **Design View** button on the Status bar and click the **Design**, **Tools**, **Add Existing Fields** button. This opens the Field List pane, shown below, containing the fields with the data for the form or report. The list shows an attachment field with a + or – sign next to it to make it expandable.

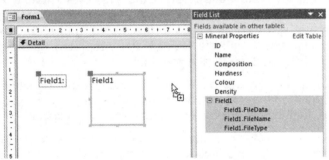

Fig. 10.11 Creating an Attachment Control

Fig. 10.11 above shows an attachment field open and selected in the Field List pane. To create the control, you drag the entire attachment field from the list to your form and drop it in the location that you want on your form, as shown. The new control (and a label) is created on your form and is bound to the table field automatically.

Note – It is critical with this operation to drag the whole field and its sub-parts as shown above, otherwise the control will not work for you. If you have problems, delete the control and try again.

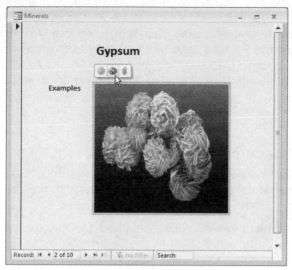

Fig. 10.12 A Working Attachment Control in Form View

Now you just re-size the control, move it to where you want on the form and save the changes. Clicking the **Form View** button on the Status bar should show the picture in the Attachment control, as in Fig. 10.12 above. This is by no means a complete Access form but it shows how the Attachment control can be used to good effect.

Fig. 10.13 Property Sheet

To change the control's properties, return to Design View, select it and then either press **F4**, or double-click the ■ button in the top-left section under the tab, or right-click and select the **Properties** option.

All of these open the Property sheet which replaces the Field List pane if it was open.

The important properties that control how your images will display in the Attachment control are **Picture Tiling**, **Picture Alignment** and **Picture Size Mode**. In our example we changed the **Picture Size Mode** setting to **Stretch** from the default **Zoom**. It worked well for us, but you always need to experiment with these settings. If you have time, you will get best results if you make all your images exactly the same size and set the control to that size.

The Attachment Toolbar

The Mini-toolbar icon [⊚ ⊚ 📎], shown in Fig. 10.12, only appears when you click the Attachment control in either Layout or Form View.

If you have multiple files attached for the record being displayed, the arrow buttons ⊙ ⊙ let you move between them. In our example, some records had several photographs attached and this is how we accessed them.

Clicking the **View Attachments** button 📎 opens the Attachments dialogue box we saw previously. This lets you add and manage your attachment files from a form.

Hypertext Links

Access 2007 and the other Office 2007 applications all support hyperlinks. A hyperlink causes a jump to another location in the current document or Web page, to a different document or Web page, or to a file that was created in a different program. You can, for example, jump from Access to a Word document to an Excel worksheet or to a PowerPoint slide to see more detail.

You can place hyperlinks in an Access 2007 database. In our example below, we have created a field to hold the Web site addresses in our Customers table.

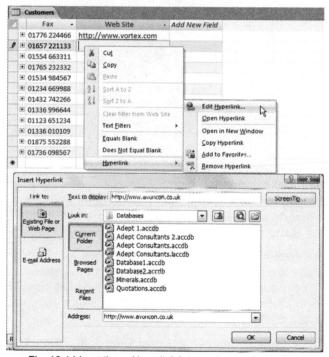

Fig. 10.14 Inserting a Hyperlink into an Access Table Cell

To do this you must first set the Data Type of the field to Hyperlink, which is easiest to do in Design View.

To enter a new hyperlink in a cell, or later to edit it, right-click the cell and select **Hyperlink**, **Edit Hyperlink** from the context menu, as shown in Fig. 10.14 on the previous page to open the Insert Hyperlink box. In our case we typed the Web address in the **Address** text box and pressed **OK**. But we could have hyperlinked to another file on our PC by selecting it in the **Look in** list.

When Access is in Datasheet or Form View, moving the pointer over a hyperlink changes it to a hand, as shown in Fig. 10.15 below. Just clicking on a hyperlink with this will jump you straight to the linked location.

Fig. 10.15 Actioning a Hyperlink in an Access Table

Sharing with Others

When you are ready to share your Access 2007 files with your friends or co-workers, there are two commands on the **Office Button** 🗐 menu for you to use.

The **Publish** command gives you options for sharing your database by publishing it to a document management server (but this requires you to use Microsoft Windows SharePoint Services), or of packaging the database, which requires you to have a digital signature.

The **E-mail** command lets you e-mail an open table or report in a variety of file formats, as shown in Fig. 10.16 on the next page.

Fig. 10.16 Choosing a File Format for E-mailing an Access Object

This is a very easy way of sharing your data. If you want to try it out, we suggest you first use your own e-mail address so that you can check what is actually being sent.

Publish as PDF or XPS

You can download a free, add-in utility from the Microsoft Download Center that lets you save or send your files in **.pdf** and **.xps** formats. To get this, go to the following site:

www.microsoft.com/downloads

Follow a link to **Office** downloads and look for **2007 Microsoft Office Add-in: Microsoft Save as PDF or XPS**.

Once you have downloaded and installed this add-in, you will be able to save tables and reports as **.pdf** and **.xps** files.

These file types are saved in a paginated, finished format that others can view no matter what type of computer system they are using. This is especially useful when you want to share your work with customers or business partners or make it ready for commercial printing. You can optimise for commercial press, high-quality desktop printing, online distribution, or on-screen display. This book was sent to the printers as a **.pdf** file.

Open the table or report that you want to publish as a **.pdf** or
.xps file, and select the **Office Button** , **Save As**, **PDF or
XPS** option to open the box shown below.

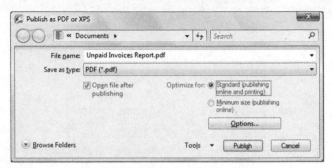

Fig. 10.17 Publishing as PDF or XPS

In the **Save as type** list, select either PDF or XPS, choose
any optimisation options and click the **Publish** button.

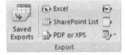
The other way to export data out of
Access is to use a command button
in the **External Data**, **Export** group.

11

Access Programming Basics

In Access 2007, programming is the process of customising your database by using Access macros or Visual Basic for Applications (VBA) code. Unlike the macros of previous versions, in Access 2007 a macro is a named collection of macro actions that you put together using the Macro Builder. It is **not** a remembered sequence of keystrokes. Macros can save a lot of time and can save mistakes creeping into your work.

In Access 2007 you can still use Microsoft Visual Basic for Applications, the programming language that is common to all Office 2007 applications. With this method, you can write quite complex Access programs. Understanding Visual Basic also makes it easier to program with other Microsoft applications that use the language. For most work however, you don't have to learn to program in Visual Basic, as the new Access Macro Builder provides plenty of power.

About Macros

In Access 97 and earlier, macros were the most common means of automating database operations. In versions 2000 to 2003, macros were supported but Microsoft recommended Visual Basic for Applications (VBA) to automate Access applications.

With Access 2007 things have changed. Microsoft now recommends using macros when possible as they run under more restrictive security settings than VBA code. On the negative side however, Access is the only Microsoft program to use these new macros, so the time you spend mastering them will not help you elsewhere.

New Features with 2007 Macros

In Access 2007, a macro can be 'stand alone' and be listed in the Navigation Pane – or it can be embedded in an object, such as a form, report, or a control.

For security against malicious code, Access 2007 won't allow a macro to run if it is not 'trusted', unless the database itself is opened from a trusted location on your computer.

New macro actions allow you to check for errors or view a macro one step at a time when it is run.

Temporary variables can now be used in a macro, which can also be part of VBA code.

Macros or VBA?

All database objects (such as forms, reports and controls) have a wide variety of event properties such as clicking the mouse, opening or closing a form, or modifying data in a text box, to which you can easily attach macros.

As we shall see, the new Macro Builder gives you a more structured interface than the Visual Basic Editor, enabling you to add programming to your controls and other objects without having to learn VBA code.

So macros provide an 'easy' way to take care of many programming tasks, such as opening and closing forms and running reports. You can quickly and easily tie together the objects in your database as there is little programming syntax that you have to remember. All the available actions and the arguments that go with them are listed and explained in the Macro Builder. All you have to do is get used to using it.

But the Access macro actions represent only a subset of the commands available in VBA. If you intend to create Access applications for others to use, learning to write VBA code is highly recommended.

The Command Button Wizard

Perhaps an easy place to start with programming is with the Command Button Wizard that is available for adding a command button to a form or report. The wizard walks you through the process of creating a command button that performs a specific task and creates a macro that is embedded in the **OnClick** property of the command button.

To see how it works, with a form open in Design View make sure the **Design**, **Controls**, **Use Control Wizards** toggle button ⬉ is selected (page 144). Click the **Design**, **Controls**, **Button** command ⬛ (page 140) and then click the ⁺⬜ pointer on the form where you want the command button to be placed. The Command Button Wizard starts, as shown in Fig. 11.1 below.

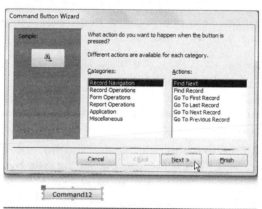

Fig. 11.1 The Command Button Wizard Opening Page

On the first page of the wizard shown above, click each category in the **Categories** list to see which **Actions** the wizard can program the command button to perform. There were 28 options for us. As you move between the available options you can see what image would show on the button for each action in the **Sample** pane on the left.

In the **Actions** list, select the action that you want, and then click the **Next** button.

The wizard will then ask you questions depending on your chosen action. We chose to **Open Form** and had to make two other selections before the page below appeared.

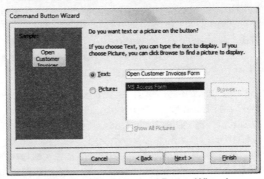

Fig. 11.2 The Command Button Wizard

Click either the **Text** option or the **Picture** option, depending on whether you want text or a picture on your command button. You can edit the text in the box next to the Text option, as we have above. If you want to select a different picture, select the **Show All Pictures** check box to display a list of all the command button pictures that Access 2007 provides, or click **Browse** to select a picture of your own. Then click **Next**.

Lastly, type a meaningful name for the new command button and click **Finish**. Access places the new button on the form, as shown in Form View for us in Fig. 11.3. It really is a painless operation.

Don't forget to save the form or you will lose you work!

Fig. 11.3 The New Command Button

If you want to see what the wizard 'programmed' for you, change back to Design View and press **F4** to display the property sheet. Click the Event tab and click the **Build** button in the **On Click** property box. Access starts the Macro Builder and displays the macro that the wizard created, as shown in Fig. 11.4 below.

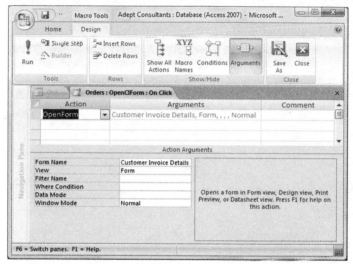

Fig. 11.4 The Command Button Code in the Macro Builder

 You can edit the macro here if you want. When you are finished, click the **Design**, **Close**, **Close** button to close the Macro Builder, saving any changes that you want to keep.

To try out the new command button, return the form to Form View and click the new button. Hopefully it will work as you expected.

The Macro Builder

To create a stand-alone macro, you open the Macro Builder by clicking the arrow below the **Create**, **Other**, **New Object** button, and selecting **Macro** from the list of three options. The other two options open the Visual Basic Editor.

The New Object button actually displays the last type of new object created, so if as in our case above, you see the Macro icon displayed, you can just click that to open the Macro Builder.

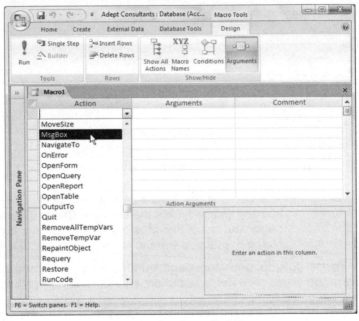

Fig. 11.5 The Macro Builder

This can be a rather daunting window at first, but please read on and persevere as the procedure of building macros in it is quite intuitive, and certainly gets easier.

In the upper part of the Macro window, from the **Action** drop-down list, you choose actions that you want the macro to carry out. In the lower **Action Arguments** pane you enter settings, or arguments, for the macro actions. The box in the lower right displays information to help you select from the action or arguments boxes, as shown below.

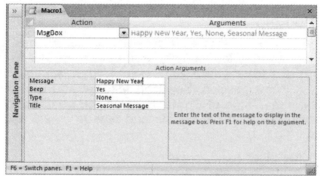

Fig. 11.6 Using Action Arguments in the Macro Builder

Here we have selected the **MsgBox** option in the **Action** list, and entered its arguments in the pane below. When the **Message** argument box was selected, instructions as to what to do were displayed in the right-hand box. As the arguments were entered in the lower pane, they were displayed in the read-only **Arguments** column above.

Fig. 11.7 Message Box

You must save a macro before you can run it. The easiest way is to click the **Save** button on the Quick Access Toolbar. After saving the macro it can be run by clicking the **Design**, **Tools**, **Run** button. Fig. 11.7 shows the resultant message box for our macro.

You can display up to five columns in the upper pane of the Macro Builder. The **Action** and **Comment** columns always show, the **Macro Names**, **Conditions**, and **Arguments** columns are controlled by clicking their toggle buttons in the **Design**, **Show/Hide** group.

In the **Action** column, you can specify any one of the default 45 macro actions provided by Access 2007. These are the actions that can all safely be used in an untrusted database. Clicking the **Design**, **Show/Hide**, **Show All Actions** button, increases the available list of actions to 70.

Macro Help

 If you click the **Microsoft Office Access Help** button in the top right of the Macro Builder window, the usual Office 2007 Help window will open in its Home position. Selecting **Macros and programm-ability** in the **Table of Contents** gives you access to all the help you will need on macros and how to create and use them.

On the other hand, pressing **F1** from the Macro Builder opens context-sensitive Help on the action currently selected, as shown in Fig. 11.8 below.

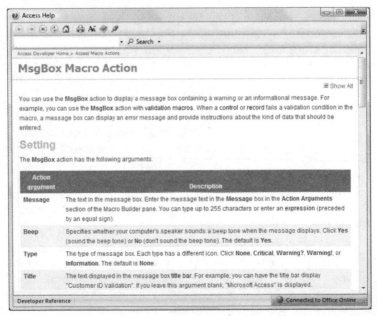

Fig. 11.8 Context Sensitive Help on a Macro Action

Each page of this help also includes examples of macro coding using the actions themselves in 'real life' database situations, as shown below. These can be invaluable when learning to program macros in Access.

Examples

Set the value of a control by using a macro

The following macro opens the Add Products form from a button on the Suppliers form. It shows the use of the **Echo**, **Close**, **OpenForm**, **SetValue**, and **GoToControl** actions. The **SetValue** action sets the Supplier ID control on the Products form to the current supplier on the Suppliers form. The **GoToControl** action then moves the focus to the Category ID field, where you can begin to enter data for the new product. This macro should be attached to the Add Products button on the Suppliers form.

Action	Arguments: Setting	Comment
Echo	Echo On: No	Stop screen updating while the macro is running.
Close	Object Type: Form	Close the Product List form.
	Object Name: Product List	
	Save: No	
OpenForm	Form Name: Products	Open the Products form.
	View: Form	
	Data Mode: Add	
	Window Mode: Normal	
SetValue	Item: [Forms]![Products]![SupplierID]	Set the Supplier ID control to the current supplier on the Suppliers form.
	Expression: SupplierID	
GoToControl	Control Name: CategoryID	Go to the Category ID control.

Fig. 11.9 A Sample Macro from Access Help

AutoExec Macro

When you open a database, Access looks for a macro with the name **AutoExec** and, if it finds one, runs it automatically. So if you create a macro and name it AutoExec it will carry out an action, or series of actions, when your database first opens.

This can be very useful if you want to open a particular form, such as a menu form to help users find their way round your database when opening Access. We will leave it to you to do this, maybe following these steps:

- Create your Menu form with command buttons pointing to the database objects you want access to.

- Create a new macro which you will name **AutoExec**.

- Select the **OpenForm** action from the **Action** list.

- Type in the name of the form – Menu – in the **Form Name** cell in the **Action Arguments** pane.

- Save the macro, exactly as AutoExec.

All being well, Access will run the macro automatically when the database is opened. Good luck.

Access Macro Security

By default, when Access 2007 opens an unknown database it disables all potentially unsafe VBA code and macros or other components, and displays the following Message Bar.

Fig. 11.10 An Access Security Warning

If you see this Message Bar, which you almost certainly will as even downloaded Microsoft templates cause it to be displayed, you first click the **Options** button.

Fig. 11.11 A VBA Macro Security Alert

This opens the Security Options box shown above. If you are doubtful of the database source just click **OK** and the code will stay disabled. If the database came from Microsoft, or you created it yourself, and you choose to trust the disabled content, you can do so in two ways:

To trust the database for the current session only, choose the **Enable this content** option shown in Fig. 11.11. With this option, you have to repeat the procedure each time you open the database.

To trust the database permanently you have to move the database to a 'trusted location'. This means a folder on a drive or network that you mark as trusted. Then, you no longer see the Message Bar as long as the database remains in the trusted folder.

Creating a Trusted Location

If you need to make a folder a trusted location, click the **Office Button** , followed by **Access Options**. On the Trust Center pane of the Access Options dialogue box, click **Trust Center Settings** to open the Trust Center dialogue box.

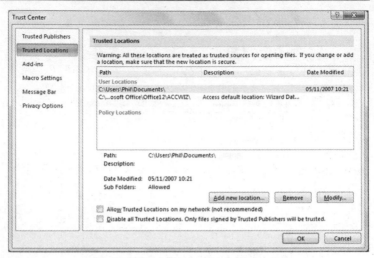

Fig. 11.12 Creating a Trusted Location

In the left pane, click Trusted Locations to show the pane above. Click the **Add new location** button and either type the file path and folder name of the location that you want to set as a trusted source, or click **Browse** to locate a folder. Click **OK** to close all open dialogue boxes.

Visual Basic Programming

You would have to use VBA programming instead of macros if you want to do any of the following:

- Use built-in functions, or create your own functions.

- Create or manipulate objects. Using VBA, you can manipulate all the objects in a database, as well as the database itself.

- Perform system-level actions.

- Manipulate records one at a time You can use VBA to step through a set of records, one record at a time, and perform an operation on each record.

An Example of VBA Code

In Access 2007 you aren't prompted to confirm any changes you make to the records on a form before the data is automatically saved. In some cases it might be useful to prompt users to confirm their changes before the record is saved. This VBA example from a Microsoft Web page does just that.

It uses a **BeforeUpdate** event procedure to display a confirmation prompt in a message box and handle the response to either cancel or continue with the save.

The first step is to load the form in Design View and press **F4** to open the Property Sheet. In the **Selection** list, select **Form** and click the Event tab to display the form's events. Click the small down-arrow in the **BeforeUpdate** event box and select **[Event Procedure]** from the drop-down list, and then click the **Build** button ⊡ next to the arrow.

This opens the Visual Basic Editor and displays the body of the **Form_BeforeUpdate** event procedure for you to add the following code, as shown in Fig. 11.13 on the next page:

```
Dim strMsg As String
Dim iResponse As Integer

' Specify the message to display.
strMsg = "Do you wish to save the changes?" & Chr(10)
strMsg = strMsg & "Click Yes to Save or No to Discard
changes."

' Display the message box.
iResponse = MsgBox(strMsg, vbQuestion + vbYesNo, "Save
Record?")

' Check the user's response.
If iResponse = vbNo Then
    ' Undo the change.
    DoCmd.RunCommand acCmdUndo

    ' Cancel the update.
    Cancel = True
End If
```

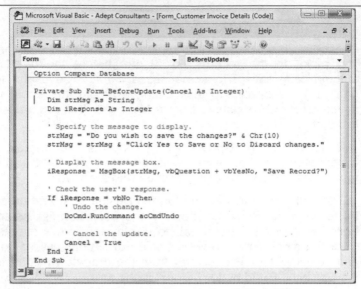

Fig. 11.13 An Event Procedure Code in VBA

If you have the time, getting to grips with Visual Basic can be very rewarding, but we're afraid that is as far as we can go here. For more help, the Visual Basic Editor has a detailed **Access Developer** help section accessed from the **Help** menu. This should keep you awake for many a long night.

****

That is about it. We hope you have enjoyed reading this book as much as we have enjoyed writing it. Of course Access 2007 is capable of a lot more than we have discussed here, but what we have tried to do is to give you enough information so that you can forge ahead and explore the rest by yourself.

Appendices listing Access Keyboard Shortcuts and data types are included next, followed by a glossary, for reference, and in case you have trouble with any jargon that may have crept in.

Appendix A

Keyboard Shortcuts

Keyboard shortcuts are single key combinations that perform a command in Access, such as **Ctrl+S** for save, or **Ctrl+B** for bold.

Key Tips on the other hand give you direct access to the Ribbon buttons, as described on page 28. When you press the **Alt** key in Access 2007, Key Tips appear in front of the Ribbon tabs and the groups and buttons on the tab. Key Tips are small indicators with a single letter or combination of letters in them, as shown below, indicating what to type to activate the control under them.

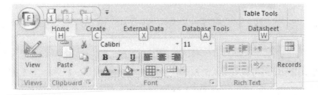

Keyboard shortcuts, however, are usually the most efficient way to perform commands with the keyboard, but of course you have to be able to remember them. Hence our listing here.

The package has an incredible number of keyboard shortcuts. In the following pages we list what we think are the most useful to remember, divided into the different aspects of Access.

We suggest you browse the listings and only attempt to memorise the shortcuts that are most useful to you.

For keyboard shortcuts in which you press two or more keys at the same time, the keys to press are separated by a plus (+) sign, for example **Ctrl+P**.

General Shortcuts

Ctrl+N	Open a new database.
Ctrl+O	Open an existing database.
Ctrl+P	Print the current or selected object.
S	Open the Page Setup dialogue box.
C or Esc	Cancel Print Preview.
Ctrl+S	Save a database object.
F12	Open the Save As dialogue box.
F11	Open and close the Navigation Pane.
Ctrl+F6	Cycle between open windows.
Alt+Space	Display the Control menu.
Shift+F10	Display the shortcut menu.
Ctrl+W or Ctrl+F4	Close the active window.
Alt+F11	Switch between the Visual Basic Editor and the previous active window.
F2	Display the complete hyperlink address for a selected hyperlink.
F7	Check spelling.
Shift+F2	Open the Zoom box to more easily enter data in small input areas.
Alt+Enter	Display a property sheet in Design view.
Alt+F4	Quit Microsoft Access.
Ctrl+F2	Invoke a Builder.

Using a Combo Box

F4	Open a combo box.
F9	Refresh the contents of a Lookup field, list box or combo box.
⇩	Move down one line.
⇧	Move up one line.
Page Down	Move down one page.
Page Up	Move up one page.
Tab	Exit a combo box or list box.

Using Find and Replace

These only work when in Datasheet and Form views.

Ctrl+F	Open the Find tab in the Find and Replace dialogue box.
Ctrl+H	Open the Replace tab in the Find and Replace dialogue box.
Shift+F4	Find the next occurrence of the specified text when the Find and Replace dialogue box is closed.

Working in Design View

F2	Switch between Edit mode when the insertion point is displayed, and Navigation mode (when an entire field is selected and the insertion point is not visible). In Navigation mode, you can move between fields with the arrow keys.
F4	Switch to the property sheet.
F5	Switch to Form view.
F6	Switch between the upper and lower portions of a window.
F7	Open the Choose Builder box.
F7	Open the Visual Basic Editor from a selected property in the property sheet.
Shift+F7	Switch from the Visual Basic Editor to form or report Design view.

Editing Controls

These shortcuts work in form and report Design view.

Ctrl+C	Copy selected control to the Clipboard.
Ctrl+X	Cut the selected control and copy it to the Clipboard.
Ctrl+V	Paste the contents of the Clipboard in the upper-left corner of the selected section.
Ctrl+⇨	Move the selected control to the right.

Ctrl+ ⇐	Move the selected control to the left.
Ctrl+ ⇧	Move the selected control up.
Ctrl+ ⇩	Move the selected control down.
Shift+ ⇩	Increase the height of the selected control.
Shift+ ⇨	Increase the width of the selected control.
Shift+ ⇧	Reduce the height of the selected control.
Shift+ ⇐	Reduce the width of the selected control.

Working with Wizards

Tab	Move the focus between wizard controls.
Alt+N	Move to the next wizard window.
Alt+B	Move to the previous wizard window.
Alt+F	Close the wizard window.

Miscellaneous

F2	Display a complete hyperlink address.
F7	Check spelling.
Shift+F2	Open the Zoom box.
Alt+Enter	Display a property sheet in Design view.
Ctrl+F2	Invoke a Builder.
Ctrl+ ⇨	Toggle forward between views when in a table, query, form, report, page, PivotTable list, PivotChart report, stored procedure, or Access project (.adp) function.
Ctrl+ ⇐	Toggle back between views when in a table, query, form, report, page, PivotTable list, PivotChart report, stored procedure, or .adp function.

Navigation Pane Shortcuts

F2	Rename a selected object.
⇩	Move down one line.
Page Down	Move down one window.
End	Move to the last object.
⇧	Move up one line.
Page Up	Move up one window.
Home	Move to the first object.
Enter	Open the selected table or query in Datasheet view.
Enter	Open the selected form or report.
Enter	Run the selected macro.
Ctrl+Enter	Open the selected table, query, form, report, data access page, macro, or module in Design view.
Ctrl+G	Display the Immediate window in the Visual Basic Editor.

Handling Text and Data

Selection Shortcuts

When selecting text in a field you can use the following shortcuts.

Shift+⇒	Extend the selection one character to the right.
Ctrl+Shift+⇒	Extend the selection one word to the right.
Shift+⇐	Extend the selection one character to the left.
Ctrl+Shift+⇐	Extend the selection one word to the left.

When selecting a field or record you can use the following shortcuts.

Tab	Select the next field.
F2	Switch between Edit mode and Navigation mode.
Shift+Space	Switch between selecting the current record and the first field of the current record, in Navigation mode.
Shift+⇧	Extend the selection to the previous record.
Shift+⇩	Extend the selection to the next record.
Ctrl+A	Select all records.

When extending a selection in Datasheet view you can use the following shortcuts.

F8	Turn on Extend mode (**Extended Selection** appears in the lower-right corner of the window). Pressing F8 repeatedly extends the selection to the word, the field, the record, and all records.
⇐ or ⇒	Extend a selection to adjacent fields.
⇧ or ⇩	Extend a selection to adjacent rows.
Shift+F8	Undo the previous extension.
Esc	Cancel Extend mode.

When selecting and moving a column in Datasheet view you can use the following shortcuts.

Ctrl+Space	Select the current column or cancel the column selection, in Navigation mode.
Shift+⇒	Select the column to the right.
Shift+⇐	Select the column to the left.
Ctrl+Shift+F8	Turn on Move mode in which you can move selected columns using ⇒ or ⇐.

Editing Shortcuts

Don't forget that if the insertion point is not visible you can press F2 to display it.

When moving the insertion point in a field:

⇨	Move the insertion point one character to the right.
Ctrl+⇨	Move the insertion point one word to the right.
⇦	Move the insertion point one character to the left
Ctrl+⇦	Move the insertion point one word to the left.
End	Move the insertion point to the end of the field, in single-line fields.
Ctrl+End	Move the insertion point to the end of the field, in multiple-line fields.
Home	Move the insertion point to the beginning of the field, in single-line fields.
Ctrl+Home	Move the insertion point to the beginning of the field, in multiple-line fields.

When copying, moving, or deleting text:

Ctrl+C	Copy the selection to the Clipboard.
Ctrl+X	Cut the selection and copy it to the Clipboard.
Ctrl+V	Paste the contents of the Clipboard at the insertion point.
Backspace	Delete the selection, or the character, to the left of the insertion point.
Delete	Delete the selection or the character, to the right of the insertion point.
Ctrl+Delete	Delete all characters to the right of the insertion point.

When you want to undo changes you have made:

Ctrl+Z	Undo typing.
Esc	Undo changes in the current field or record.

When entering data in Datasheet or Form view:

Ctrl+;	Insert the current date.
Ctrl+Shift+:	Insert the current time.
Ctrl+Alt+Space	Insert the default value for a field.
Ctrl+'	Insert the value from the same field in the previous record.
Ctrl+Plus sign	Add a new record.
Ctrl+Minus sign	Delete the current record.
Shift+Enter	Save changes to the current record.
Space	Switch between the values in a check box or option button.
Ctrl+Enter	Insert a new line.

When refreshing fields with current data:

F9	Recalculate the fields in the window, or the contents of a Lookup field, list box or combo box.
Shift+F9	Rerun a query so as to reflect changes to the records.

Navigating Records

Design View

F2	Switch between Edit mode (with insertion point displayed) and Navigation mode.
F4	Toggle the property sheet.
F5	Switch to Form view, when in form Design view.

F6	Switch between the upper and lower portions of a window.
F7	Open the Visual Basic Editor from a selected property in the property sheet for a form or report.
Alt+F8	Open the Field List pane in a form, report , or data access page. If the Field List pane is already open it moves the focus to it.
Shift+F7	With a code module open, switch from the Visual Basic Editor to form or report Design view.
Shift+F7	Switch from a control's property sheet in form or report Design view to the design surface, without changing the focus.
Alt+Enter	Display a property sheet in Design view.
Ctrl+C	Copy the selected control to the Clipboard.
Ctrl+X	Cut the selected control and copy it to the Clipboard.
Ctrl+V	Paste the contents of the Clipboard in the upper-left corner of the selected section.
⇨ or ⇦	Move the selected control to the right or left by one pixel along the page grid.
⇧ or ⇩	Move the selected control up or down by one pixel along the page grid
Ctrl+⇨ or ⇦	Move the selected control to the right or left by one pixel ignoring the page grid.
Ctrl+⇧ or ⇩	Move the selected control up or down by one pixel ignoring the page grid.
Shift+⇨ or ⇦	Increase or decrease the width of the selected control to the right or left by one pixel.
Shift+⇧ or ⇩	Decrease or increase the height of the selected control from the bottom or top by one pixel.

Datasheet View

Some of these shortcuts will only work when you are in Navigation mode.

F5	Move to the record number box, type a number in the box, and press Enter.
Tab or ⇨	Move to the next field.
End	Move to the last field in the current record.
Shift+Tab, or ⇦	Move to the previous field.
Home	Move to the first field in the current record.
⇩	Move to the current field in the next record.
Ctrl+⇩	Move to the current field in the last record.
Ctrl+End	Move to the last field in the last record.
⇧	Move to the current field in the previous record.
Ctrl+⇧	Move to the current field in the first record.
Ctrl+Home	Move to the first field in the first record.
Page Down	Go down one screen.
Page Up	Go up one screen.
Ctrl+Page Down	Go right one screen.
Ctrl+Page Up	Go left one screen.

Form View

F5	Move to the record number box which displays the current record number in the lower-left corner. To move to another record, you can type its number in the box, and press **Enter**.
Tab	Move to the next field.
Shift+Tab	Move to the previous field .
End	Move to the last field in the current record.
Ctrl+End	Move to the last field in the last record.
Home	Move to the first field in the current record.
Ctrl+Home	Move to the first field in the first record.
Ctrl+Page Down	Move to the current field in the next record.

Ctrl+Page Up	Move to the current field in the previous record.
Page Down	Go down one page. At the end of a record it moves to the equivalent page on the next record.
Page Up	Go up one page. At the end of a record it moves to the equivalent page on the previous record.

When navigating between the main form and subform.

Tab	Enter the subform from the preceding field in the main form.
Shift+Tab	Enter the subform from the following field in the main form.
Ctrl+Tab	Exit the subform and move to the next field in the master form or next record.
Ctrl+Shift+Tab	Exit the subform and move to the previous field in the main form or previous record.

Print Preview and Layout Preview

P or Ctrl+P	Open the Print dialogue box.
S	Open the Page Setup dialogue box.
Z	Zoom in or out on a part of the page.
C or Esc	Cancel Print Preview or Layout Preview.
Alt+F5	Move to the page number box.
Page Down or ⇩	View the next page.
Page Up or ⇧	View the previous page.
⇩	Scroll down in small increments.
Page Down	Scroll down one full screen.
Ctrl+ ⇩	Move to the bottom of the page.
⇧	Scroll up in small increments.
Page Up	Scroll up one full screen.
Ctrl+ ⇧	Move to the top of the page.
⇨	Scroll to the right in small increments.
End	Move to the right edge of the page.

Ctrl+End	Move to the lower-right corner of the page.
⇐	Scroll to the left in small increments.
Home	Move to the left edge of the page.
Ctrl+Home	Move to the upper-left corner of the page.

PivotTable View

This is an Access view that summarises and analyses data in a datasheet or form.

F1	Display Help topics.
Shift+F10	Display the shortcut menu for the selected element of the PivotTable view.
Esc	Close the shortcut menu without carrying out a command.
Alt+Enter	Display the Properties dialogue box.
Alt+F4	Close the Properties dialogue box.
Ctrl+C	Copy the selected data from the Pivot-Table view to the Clipboard.
Ctrl+E	Export the contents of the PivotTable view to Microsoft Excel.
Ctrl+8	Show or hide the expand indicators beside items.
Ctrl+Plus sign	Expand the currently selected item.
Ctrl+Minus sign	Hide the currently selected item.
Alt+⇓	Open the list for the currently selected field.
Ctrl+T	Turn AutoFilter on or off.
Ctrl+Shift+A	Sort data in the selected field or total in ascending order.
Ctrl+Shift+Z	Sort data in the selected field or total in descending order.
Alt+Shift+⇑	Move the selected member up.
Alt+Shift+⇐	Move the selected member left.
Alt+Shift+⇓	Move the selected member down.

Alt+Shift+⇨	Move the selected member right.
Ctrl+L	Display or activate the field list.
⇧, ⇩, ⇦ or ⇨	Move to the next item in the field list.
Shift+⇧	Move to the previous item and include it in the selection.
Shift+⇩	Move to the next item and include it in the selection.
Ctrl+⇧	Move to the previous item, but do not include the item in the selection.
Ctrl+⇩	Move to the next item, but do not include the item in the selection.
Ctrl+Space	Remove the item from the selection.
Plus sign	Expand the current item in the Field List pane to display its contents.
Minus sign	Collapse the current item in the Field List pane to hide its contents.
Tab	Alternately, move to the most recently selected item, the **Add to** button, and the list next to the **Add to** button in the Field List pane.
Alt+⇩	Open the drop-down list next to the **Add to** button in the Field List pane. Use the arrow keys to move to the next item in the list, and then press ENTER to select an item.
Enter	Add the highlighted field in the Field List pane to the area in the PivotTable view that is displayed in the **Add to** list.
Alt+F4	Close the Field List pane.
Ctrl+Shift+S	Add a new total field using the Sum summary function.
Ctrl+Shift+C	Add a new total field using the Count summary function.
Ctrl+Shift+M	Add a new total field using the Min summary function.
Ctrl+Shift+X	Add a new total field using the Max summary function.

Ctrl+Shift+E	Add a new total field using the Average summary function.
Ctrl+Shift+D	Add a new total field using the Standard Deviation summary function.
Ctrl+Shift+T	Add a new total field using the Standard Deviation Population summary function.
Ctrl+Shift+V	Add a new total field using the Variance summary function.
Ctrl+Shift+R	Add a new total field using the Variance Population summary function.
Ctrl+Shift+B	Turn subtotals and grand totals on or off for the selected field.
Ctrl+F	Add a calculated detail field.
Ctrl+1	Move the selected field to the row area.
Ctrl+2	Move the selected field to the column area.
Ctrl+3	Move the selected field to the filter area.
Ctrl+4	Move the selected field to the detail area.
Ctrl+ ⇐	Move the selected row or column field to a higher level.
Ctrl+ ⇒	Move the selected row or column field to a lower level.

Formatting Elements

To use these shortcut keys for formatting elements in PivotTable view, first select a detail field or a data cell for a total field.

Ctrl+Shift+~	Apply the general number format.
Ctrl+Shift+$	Apply the currency format, with two decimal places and negative numbers in parentheses.
Ctrl+Shift+%	Apply the percentage format, with no decimal places.
Ctrl+Shift+^	Apply the exponential number format, with two decimal places.
Ctrl+Shift+#	Apply the date format, with the day, month, and year.

Ctrl+Shift+@	Apply the time format, with the hour, minute, and AM or PM.
Ctrl+Shift+!	Apply the numeric format, with two decimal places, thousands separator, and a minus sign for negative values.
Ctrl+B	Make selected text bold.
Ctrl+U	Make selected text underlined.
Ctrl+I	Make selected text italic.

The Help Window

F1	Open the Help window.
Alt+F4	Close the Help window.
Alt+Tab	Switch between the Help window and Access.
Alt+Home	Go back to Access Home.
Tab	Select the next item in the Help window.
Shift+Tab	Select the previous item.
Enter	Perform the action for the selected item.
Tab, Shift+Tab	Select the next or previous item.
Alt+ ⇐	Move back to the previous Help topic.
Alt+ ⇒	Move forward to the next Help topic.
⇧ or ⇩	Scroll small amounts up or down within the currently displayed Help topic.
Page Up or Down	Scroll larger amounts up or down within the currently displayed Help topic.
Shift+F10	Display a menu of commands for the (active) Help window.
Esc	Stop the last action.
F5	Refresh the window.
Ctrl+P	Print the current Help topic.
F6	Switch among areas in the Help window.

Appendix B

Access 2007 Data Types

The following tables describe the data types and properties available for fields in Access 2007.

Data Type	Information Stored and Size
Text	Alphanumeric characters. Use for text, or text and numbers that are not used in calculations. Up to 255 characters.
Memo	Alphanumeric characters (longer than 255 characters) or text with rich text formatting. Up to 1 GB (gigabyte) of characters, or 2 GB of storage, of which you can display 65,535 characters in a control.
Number	Numeric values (integers or fractional values). Use for storing numbers to be used in calculations, except for money values. 1, 2, 4, or 8 bytes, or 16 bytes when used for replication ID.
Date/Time	Dates and times. Use for storing date/time values. Each value stored includes both a date component and a time component. 8 bytes.
Currency	Monetary values. Use for storing monetary values. 8 bytes.

AutoNumber	A unique numeric value that Access 2007 automatically inserts when a record is added.
	Use for generating unique values that can be used as a primary key. AutoNumber fields can be incremented sequentially, by a specified increment, or chosen randomly.
	4 bytes or 16 bytes when used for replication ID.
Yes/No	Boolean values.
	Use for True/False fields that can hold one of two possible values, such as Yes/No or True/False.
	1 bit (8 bits = 1 byte).
OLE Object	OLE objects or other binary data.
	Use for storing OLE objects from other Microsoft Windows applications.
	Up to 1 GB.
Attachment	Pictures, Images, Binary files, Office files. This is the preferred data type for storing digital images and any type of binary file.
	For compressed attachments, 2 GB. For uncompressed attachments, approx. 700k, depending on the degree of compression.
Hyperlink	Hyperlinks.
	Use for storing hyperlinks to provide single-click access to Web pages through a URL (Uniform Resource Locator) or files through a name in UNC (universal naming convention) format.
	Up to 1 GB of characters, or 2 GB of storage (2 bytes per character), of which you can display 65,535 characters in a control.

Lookup Wizard | Not actually a data type, but invokes the Lookup Wizard.
Use to start the Lookup Wizard so you can create a field that uses a combo box to look up a value in another table, query or list of values.

Field Properties

Access uses the field property settings when you view and edit data. They do such things as, controlling the appearance of information, preventing incorrect entries, specifying default values, or speeding up searching and sorting. The data type of the field determines the properties you can set.

Property	*Description*
Field Size	Sets the maximum size for data stored as a Text, Number, or AutoNumber data type. See next section.
Format	Customises the way the field appears when displayed or printed.
DecimalPlaces	Specifies the number of decimal places to use when displaying numbers.
NewValues	Sets whether an AutoNumber field is incremented or assigned a random value.
InputMask	Displays editing characters to guide data entry.
Caption	Sets the text displayed by default in labels for forms, reports, and queries.
DefaultValue	Automatically assigns a default value to a field when new records are added.

ValidationRule	Supplies an expression that must be true whenever you add or change the value in this field.
ValidationText	Enters text that appears when a value violates the ValidationRule expression.
Required	Requires that data be entered in a field.
AllowZeroLength	Allows the entry (by setting to Yes) of a zero-length string ("") in a Text or Memo field.
Indexed	Speeds up access to data in this field by creating and using an index.
UnicodeCompression	Compresses text stored in this field when over 4,096 characters are stored.
SmartTags	Attaches a smart tag to this field.
AppendOnly	Allows versioning (by setting to Yes) of a Memo field.
TextFormat	Chooses Rich Text to store text as HTML and allows rich formatting. Chooses Plain Text to store only text.
TextAlign	Specifies the default alignment of text within a control.
Precision	Specifies the total number of digits allowed, including those both to the right and the left of the decimal point.
Scale	Specifies the maximum number of digits that can be stored to the right of the decimal separator.

Field Size Properties

Some additional information about the FieldSize properties.

Field Size Property Description

Text

Enter a value from 1 to 255. Text fields can range from 1 to 255 characters.

Number

Select one of the following:

Byte – For numeric values that range from 0 to 255. Storage requirement is a single byte.

Integer – For numeric values that range from –32,768 to +32,768. Storage requirement is two bytes.

Long Integer – For numeric values that range from –2,147,483,648 to +2,147,483,647. Storage requirement is four bytes.

Single – For numeric floating point values that range from -3.4×10^{38} to $+3.4 \times 10^{38}$ and up to seven significant digits. Storage requirement is four bytes.

Double – For numeric floating point values that range from -1.797×10^{308} to $+1.797 \times 10^{308}$ and up to fifteen significant digits. Storage requirement is eight bytes.

Replication ID – For storing a globally unique identifier required for replication. Storage requirement is sixteen bytes.

Decimal – For numeric values that range from $-9.999... \times 10^{27}$ to $+9.999... \times 10^{27}$. Storage requirement is twelve bytes.

AutoNumber Select one of the following:

Long Integer – For unique, numeric values that range from 1 to +2,147,483,648 when the New Values field property is set to Increment, and –2,147,483,648 to +2,147,483,647 when the New Values field property is set to Random. Storage requirement is four bytes.

Replication ID – For storing a globally unique identifier required for replication. Storage requirement is sixteen bytes.

Format Properties

Some additional information about the Format properties.

Property	*Comments*
Number	Select one of the following:

General Number – Displays the number as entered.

Currency – Displays the number using the thousand separator, and applies the settings in the Regional and Language Options in the Control Panel for negative amounts, decimal and currency symbols, and decimal places. E.g., 3456.789 becomes £3,456.79

Euro – Displays the number using the Euro currency symbol, regardless of the symbol specified in the Regional and Language Options.

Fixed – Displays at least one digit and applies the settings in the Regional

and Language Options in the Control Panel for negative amounts, decimal and currency symbols, and decimal places.
E.g., 3456.789 becomes 3456.79

Standard – Displays the number using the thousand separator and applies the settings in the Regional and Language Options in the Control Panel for negative amounts, decimal symbols, and decimal places. This format does not display a currency symbol.
E.g., 3456.789 becomes 3,456.79

Percent – Multiplies the value by 100 and displays the number with a percent sign added to the end. Applies the settings in the Regional and Language Options in the Control Panel for negative amounts, decimal symbols, and decimal places.
E.g., 0.3456 becomes 35%

Scientific – Displays the value in standard scientific notation.
E.g., 3456.789 becomes 3.46E+03

Date/Time

Select one of the following predefined display formats:

General Date – Displays the value using a combination of the Short Date and Long Time settings.

Long Date – Displays the value using the Long Date setting from the Regional and Language Options settings in the Control Panel.

Medium Date – Displays the value using the format dd-mmm-yy (14-Jul-07, for example).

Short Date – Displays the value using the Short Date setting from the Regional and Language Options in the Control Panel.

Long Time – Displays the value using the Time setting in the Regional and Language Options in the Control Panel.

Medium Time – Displays the value using the format HH:MM PM where HH is the hour, MM is the minute, and PM is either AM or PM. The hour can range from 1 to 12. The minute can range from 0 to 59.

Short Time – Displays the value using the format HH:MM where HH is the hour and MM is the minute. The hour can range from 0 to 23 and the minute from 0 to 59.

Yes/No   Select one of the following:

True/False – Displays the value as either True or False.

Yes/No – Displays the value as either Yes or No.

On/Off – Displays the value as either On or Off.

Glossary of Terms

Access database
: A collection of data and objects (such as tables, queries, or forms) that is related to a particular topic or purpose.

Action
: The basic building block of an Access 2007 macro.

Active
: Describes the folder, window or icon that you are currently using or that is currently selected.

Action query
: An Access query that copies or changes data, identified by an exclamation mark (!) next to its name in the Navigation Pane.

Add-in
: A mini-program which runs in conjunction with another and enhances its functionality.

ADE file
: An Access project (**.accdp**) file with all modules compiled and all editable source code removed.

Append query
: An action query that adds the records in a query's result set to the end of an existing table.

Application
: Software (program) designed to carry out certain activity, such as word processing or data manipulation.

Autoformat
: A collection of formats that determines the appearance of the controls and sections in an Access form or report.

AutoNumber
: An Access field data type that automatically stores a unique

	number for each record as it is added to a table.
Backup	To make a back-up copy of a file or a disc for safekeeping.
Bigint	An Access data type of 8 bytes (64 bits).
Binary	A fixed-length Access data type with a maximum of 8,000 bytes of binary data.
Bit	An Access data type that stores either a 1 or 0 value. Integer values other than 1 or 0 are accepted, but they are always interpreted as 1.
Bound column	The column in an Access list box, combo box, or drop-down list box that is bound to the field specified by the control's **ControlSource** property.
Bound control	A control used on an Access form or report to display or modify data from a table, query, or SQL statement. The **ControlSource** property stores the field name to which the control is bound.
Broadband	A communications systems in which the medium of transmission (such as a wire or fibre-optic cable) carries multiple messages.
Browse	A button in some Windows dialogue boxes that lets you view a list of files and folders before you make a selection. Also to view a Web page.

Browser	A program, like Internet Explorer, that lets you view Web pages.
Builder	An Access tool that simplifies a task, such as the Expression Builder.
Button	A graphic element or icon in a dialogue box or toolbar that performs a specified function.
Byte	An Access data type that is used to hold small positive integers ranging from 0 to 255. Or a unit of data that holds a single character, such as a letter, a digit.
Calculated control	Used on an Access form or report to display the result of an expression.
Calculated field	An Access field, defined in a query, that displays the result of an expression rather than displaying stored data.
CD-R	Recordable compact disc.
CD-ROM	Compact Disc – Read Only Memory; an optical disc which information may be read from but not written to.
CD-RW	Rewritable compact disc. Data can be copied to the CD on more than one occasion and can be erased.
Char	A fixed-length data type with a maximum of 8,000 ANSI characters.

Character code	A number that represents a particular character in a set, such as the ANSI character set.
Chart	A graphical representation of data in a form or report.
Check box	A control that indicates whether an option is selected. A check mark appears in the box when the option is selected.
Class module	A module that can contain the definition for a new object. Each instance of a class creates a new object. Procedures defined in the module become properties and methods of the object. Class modules can exist alone or with forms and reports.
Client	A computer that has access to services over a computer network. The computer providing the services is a server.
Clipboard	A temporary storage area of memory, where text and graphics are stored with the cut and copy actions. The Office clipboard can store up to 24 items.
Code stub	A segment of Visual Basic code that defines the beginning and end of a procedure.
Column	A location within a database table that stores a particular type of data. It is also the visual representation of a field in a datasheet and, in an Access database, the query design grid or the filter design grid.

Combo box	A control used on a form that provides the combined functionality of a list box and a text box.
Command	An instruction given to a computer to carry out a particular action.
Command button	A control that in Access runs a macro, calls a Visual Basic function, or runs an event procedure.
Compound control	A control and an attached label.
Configuration	A general purpose term referring to the way you have your computer set up.
Constraint	A restriction placed on the value that can be entered into a column or a row.
Context menu	A menu that opens when you right-click the mouse button on a feature.
Controls	Objects on an Access form or report that display data, perform actions, or are used for decoration.
Cookies	Files stored on your hard drive by your Web browser that hold information for it to use.
Currency	An Access data type used for calculations involving money.
Current record	The record in an Access recordset from which you can modify or retrieve data.
Database	A collection of data related to a particular topic or purpose.

Datasheet view — An Access view that displays data from a table, form, query, view, or stored procedure in a row and column format.

Date/Time — A data type that is used to hold date and time information.

DBMS — Database management system – A software interface between the database and the user.

Declaration — VBA code that names a constant, variable, or procedure, and specifies its characteristics, such as data type.

Default property — A property that you can set for a control so that each time a new control of that type is created, the property will have the same value.

Default value — A value that is automatically entered in a field or control when you add a new record.

Delete query — An Access query that removes rows matching the criteria that you specify from one or more tables.

Design grid — The grid that you use to design a query or filter in query Design view or in the Advanced Filter/Sort window. For queries, this grid is also known as the QBE grid.

Design view — An Access view that shows the design of tables, queries, forms, reports, and macros.

Desktop — The Windows screen working background.

Detail section — Used to contain the main body of an Access form or report. This section usually contains controls bound to the fields in the record source.

Device driver	A special file that must be loaded into memory for Windows to be able to address a specific procedure or hardware device.
Device name	A logical name used by an operating system to identify a device, such as LPT1 or COM1 for the parallel or serial printer.
Dialogue box	A window displayed on the screen to allow the user to enter information.
Directory	An area on disc where information relating to a group of files is kept. Also known as a folder.
Disc	A device on which you can store programs and data.
Document	A file produced by an application program.
Domain	A group of devices, servers and computers on a network.
Double-click	To quickly press and release a mouse button twice.
Double precision	Characteristic of a number stored in twice the amount (two words; typically 8 bytes) of computer memory that is required for storing a less precise (single-precision) number. Commonly handled by a computer in floating-point form.
Download	To transfer to your computer a file, or data, from the Internet, or another computer.

Drag	To move an object on the screen by pressing and holding down the left mouse button while moving the mouse.
Drive name	The letter followed by a colon which identifies a floppy or hard disc drive.
Drop-down list	A menu item that can be clicked to open extra items that can be selected.
DVD	A type of optical disc able to store at least 4.7 GB of digital data, such as software programs, photographs and full-length movies.
Dynamic-link library	A set of routines that can be called from Visual Basic procedures and are loaded and linked into your application at run time.
Echo	The process of Access updating or repainting the screen while a macro is running.
E-mail	Electronic Mail – A system that allows computer users to send and receive messages.
Embedded object	Information in a document that is 'copied' from its source application. Selecting the object opens the creating application from within the document.
Export	To copy data and database objects for use outside of Access.
Expression Builder	An Access tool that you can use to create an expression.

Field data type | A characteristic of a field that determines what kind of data it can store.

Field List pane | An Access pane that lists all the fields in the underlying record source, or database object.

File extension | The suffix following the period in a filename. Windows uses this to identify the source application program. For example **.accdb** indicates a Microsoft Access file.

Filename | The name given to a file. In Windows 95 and above this can be up to 256 characters long.

Filter | A set of criteria applied to data in order to display a subset of the data or to sort the data.

Firewall | A system that prevents unauthorised access to a computer over the internet.

Floating | Able to move freely in its own window. A floating window is always on top, such as the Expression Builder.

Floppy disc | A removable disc on which information can be stored.

Folder | An area used to store a group of files, usually with a common link.

Font | A graphic design representing a set of characters, numbers and symbols.

Form | An Access database object on which you place controls for taking actions or for entering,

	displaying, and editing data in fields.
Form selector	The box where the rulers meet, in the upper-left corner of an Access form in Design view. Used for selecting the form.
Form view	An Access view that displays a form that you use to show or accept data. Form view is the primary means of adding and modifying data in tables.
Format	Specifies how data is displayed and printed.
FTP	File Transfer Protocol. The procedure for connecting to a remote computer and transferring files.
Function	A query that takes input parameters and returns a result like a stored procedure.
Function key	One of the series of 10 or 12 keys marked with the letter F and a numeral, used for specific operations.
Function procedure	In VBA, a procedure that returns a value and that can be used in an expression.
Gigabyte	(GB); 1,024 megabytes. Usually thought of as one billion bytes.
Graphic	A picture or illustration, also called an image. Formats include GIF, JPEG, BMP, PCX, and TIFF.
Grid	In Datasheet view – Vertical and horizontal lines that visually divide rows and columns of data into

	cells in a table, query, form, view, or stored procedure.
	In Design view – An arrangement of vertical and horizontal dotted and solid lines that help you position controls precisely when you design a form or report.
Hard copy	Output on paper.
Hard disc	A device built into the computer for holding programs and data.
Hardware	The equipment that makes up a computer system, excluding the programs or software.
Help	A Windows system that gives you instructions and additional information on using a program.
HTML	HyperText Markup Language, the format used in documents on the Web.
Hyperlink	A data type for an Access database field that stores hyperlink addresses.
Hyperlink address	The path to a destination such as an object, document, or Web page.
Icon	A small graphic image, or button, that represents a function or object. Clicking on an icon produces an action.
Image	See graphic.
Image control	A control that is used to display a picture on an Access form or report.

Import	To copy data from a text file, spreadsheet file, or database table into an Access table.
Input mask	A format that consists of literal display characters and mask characters that specify where data is to be entered, the kind of data and how many characters are allowed.
Insertion point	A flashing bar that shows where typed text will be entered into a document.
Int	An Access data type of 4 bytes (32 bits).
Integer	An Access data type that holds integers.
Interface	A device that allows you to connect a computer to its peripherals.
JPEG/JPG	Joint Photographic Experts Group, a popular cross-platform format for image files – best suited for true colour original images.
Kilobyte	(KB); 1024 bytes of information or storage space.
Label	A control that displays descriptive text, such as a title, a caption, or instructions, on an Access form or report.
Layout view	In Access 2007, a view in which you can make many types of design changes to forms and reports while viewing live data.

Linked table	A table stored in a file outside the open database from which Access can access records.
Links	Hypertext connections between Web pages.
Lookup field	A field, used on an Access form or report that either displays a list of values retrieved from a table or query, or a stored set of values.
Macro	An action or set of actions that you can use to automate tasks.
Macro Builder	The window in which you create and modify macros.
Make-table query	A query that creates a new table and then creates records (rows) in that table by copying records from an existing table or query results.
Malware	Generic term for software designed to perform harmful or surreptitious acts on a computer.
Megabyte	(MB); 1024 kilobytes of information or storage space.
Megahertz	(MHz); Speed of processor in millions of cycles per second.
Memo	An Access field data type. Memo fields can contain up to 65,535 characters.
Module level	Describes any variable or constant declared in the Declarations section of a VBA module.
Monitor	The display device connected to your PC, also called a screen.

Mouse	A device used to move a pointer around and activate processes by pressing buttons.
Move mode	The mode in which you can move a column in Datasheet view by using the left and right arrow keys.
Multimedia	The use of photos, sound and movie images in a presentation.
Navigation buttons	The buttons that you use to move through records. They are located in the lower left corner of the Datasheet and Form views.
Navigation Pane	The pane that appears when you open an Access database or project. The Navigation Pane displays the objects in the database.
Nchar	A fixed-length Access data type with a maximum of 4,000 Unicode characters.
Network	Two or more computers connected together to share resources.
Normalise	To minimise the duplication of information in a relational database. You can use the Table Analyzer Wizard to normalise your database.
Ntext	A variable-length Access data type.
Number	An Access field data type designed for numerical data that will be used in mathematical calculations.

Numeric	An exact numeric Access data type that holds values from $-10^{38}-1$ to $10^{38}-1$.
Office Suite	A bundle of useful programs sold in one package, like Office 2007.
OLE	Object Linking and Embedding – A technology for transferring and sharing information among software applications.
OLE container	A program that contains a linked or embedded OLE object from another program. For example, if an OLE object in an Access database contains an Excel worksheet, Access is the OLE container.
OLE server	A program or DLL that supplies a linked or embedded OLE object to another program.
One-to-many	An association (relationship) between two tables in which the primary key value of each record in the primary table corresponds to the value in the matching field or fields of many records in the related table.
One-to-one	An association between two tables in which the primary key value of each record in the primary table corresponds to the value in the matching field or fields of one, and only one, record in the related table.
Option button	A control, also called a radio button, that is typically used as part of an option group to present alternatives on a form or report.

PDF	Portable Document Format. A file format developed by Adobe that allows formatted pages of text and graphics to be viewed and printed correctly on any computer with a PDF Reader.
Peripheral	Any device attached to a PC.
PivotChart view	A view that shows a graphical analysis of data in a datasheet or form. You can see different levels of detail or specify the layout by dragging fields and items or by showing and hiding items in the drop-down lists for the fields.
PivotTable form	An interactive table that summarises large amounts of data by using format and calculation methods that you choose.
PivotTable view	A view that summarises and analyses data in an Access datasheet or form.
Pixel	A picture element on screen; the smallest element that can be independently assigned colour and intensity.
Primary key 🔑	One or more fields (columns) whose values uniquely identify each record in an Access table.
Procedure	A sequence of declarations and statements in a VBA module that are executed as a unit.
Program	A set of instructions which cause a computer to perform tasks.
Project	The set of all code modules in a database, including standard

	modules and class modules. By default, the project has the same name as the database.
Property sheet	A pane that is used to view or modify the properties of objects such as Access tables, queries, fields, forms, reports and controls.
Publish	To save a database to a document management server, such as a server running Windows SharePoint Services.
QBE grid	The **Q**uery **b**y **E**xample grid that you use to design a query or filter in query Design view. Also known as the design grid.
Query	A question about the data stored in your tables, or a request to perform an action on the data. A query can bring together data from multiple Access tables to serve as the source of data for a form or report.
Query window	An Access window in which you work with queries in Design view, Datasheet view, SQL view, or Print Preview.
Radio button	A method of selecting an option in an application dialogue box – also called an Option button.
RAM	Random Access Memory. The computer's volatile memory. Data held in it is lost when power is switched off.
Referential integrity	Rules that you follow to preserve the defined relationships between

	tables when you add, update, or delete records.
Refresh	In an Access database, to redisplay the records in a form or datasheet to reflect changes that other users have made.
Relationship	An association that is established between common fields (columns) in two tables. A relationship can be one-to-one, one-to-many, or many-to-many.
Report	An Access database object containing information that is formatted and organised according to your specifications for printing.
ROM	Read Only Memory. A PC's non-volatile memory. Data is written into this memory at manufacture and is not affected by power loss.
RTF	Rich Text Format. A common file format used to transfer files between different programs. It preserves most of the formatting of a document.
Select query	An Access query that asks a question about the data stored in your tables and returns a result set in the form of a datasheet, without changing the data.
Shortcut	A link to any item accessible on your computer or on a network, such as a program, file, folder, disc drive, Web page, printer, or another computer.

Smalldatetime	A date and time Access data type that is less precise than the datetime data type.
Smallint	An Access data type of 2 bytes (16 bits).
Smallmoney	An Access data type that stores monetary values. When smallmoney values are displayed, they are rounded up to two decimal places.
Software	The programs and instructions that control your PC.
SQL database	A database that is based on Structured Query Language (SQL).
SQL statement	An expression that defines a SQL command.
SQL view	An Access window that displays the SQL statement for the current query. When you create a query in Design view, Access constructs the SQL equivalent in SQL view.
Standard deviation	A parameter that indicates the way in which a probability function is centred around its mean. The square root of the average of the squared differences between data points and the mean.
Standard module	A VBA module in which you can place Sub and Function procedures that you want to be available to other procedures throughout your database.
Sub procedure	A VBA procedure that carries out an operation. Unlike a Function

	procedure, a Sub procedure doesn't return a value.
Subform	A form contained within another Access form or a report.
Sysname	A special system-supplied, user-defined data type that is used for table columns, variables, and stored procedure parameters that store object names.
System object	Database objects that are defined by the system, such as the table MSysIndexes, or by the user. You can create a system object by naming the object with USys as the first four characters in the object name.
Table	A database object that stores data in records (rows) and fields (columns). The data is usually about a particular category of things, such as employees or orders.
Table properties	Attributes of an Access table that affect the appearance or behaviour of the table as a whole. Table properties are set in table Design view, as are field properties.
Task Pane	A pane or sub-window that gives a range of options pertaining to the task currently being performed.
Template	A page design, document, spreadsheet or database, that contains all the required formatting for a particular style or type of document.

Text	An Access variable-length data type.
Text box	A control used on a form or report to display text or accept data entry. A text box can have a label attached to it.
Text file	An unformatted file of text characters saved in ASCII format.
Tinyint	An Access data type of 1 byte (8 bits) that stores whole numbers in the range of 0 through 255.
Toggle	To turn an action on and off with the same switch.
Toggle button	A control that is used to provide on/off options on a form or report.
Toolbox	A set of Access tools available in the **Design**, **Controls** group when in Design view, for adding controls to a form or report.
ToolTips	Brief descriptions of the names of commands and buttons on the Ribbon. A ToolTip is displayed when the mouse pointer rests on these commands and buttons.
Total row	A row on a datasheet that displays your choice of summary information for each field, based on the type of data in the field.
Totals query	An Access query that displays a summary calculation, such as an average or sum, for values in various fields from a table or tables.
Unbound control	A control that is not connected to a field in an underlying table, query, or SQL statement. An

	unbound control is often used to display informational text or decorative pictures.
Union query	An Access query that uses the UNION operator to combine the results of two or more select queries.
Update	To accept changes to data in a record. The changes are saved in the database when you move to another record on a form or datasheet, or when you explicitly save the record.
Update query	An action query that changes a set of records according to criteria that you specify.
URL	Uniform Resource Locator, the addressing system used on the Web, containing information about the method of access, the server to be accessed and the path of the file to be accessed.
User defined type	In VBA, any data type defined by using the Type statement.
Validation	The process of checking whether entered data meets certain conditions or limitations.
Varchar	A variable-length Access data type with a maximum of 8,000 ANSI characters.
Variance	The square of the standard deviation. It is a measure of the amount by which all values in a group vary from the average value of the group.

VBA	Visual Basic for Applications. An event driven programming language built into most Microsoft Office applications.
Web	A network of hypertext-based multimedia information servers. Browsers are used to view any information on the Web.
Web Page	An HTML document that is accessible on the Web.
Wildcard characters	Characters used in queries and expressions to include all records, file names, or other items that begin with specific characters or that match a certain pattern.
Wizard	A Microsoft tool that steps you through certain operations, or asks you questions and then creates an object depending on your answers.
XPS	(XML Paper Specification) is Microsoft's answer to the Adobe PDF file format. It describes electronic paper in a way that can be read by hardware, software, and by humans. Microsoft has integrated XPS into Office 2007 and the Windows Vista operating system, but XPS itself is platform independent, openly published, and available royalty-free.
Yes/No	An Access data type that you use for fields that will contain only one of two values, such as Yes or No and True or False. Null values are not allowed.

Zero-length string   A string that contains no characters. You can use a zero-length string to indicate that you know no value exists for a field.

Index